HOODOO FOR BEGINNERS

DISCOVER THE HIDDEN PLANTS POWERS AND CONJURE WITH HERBS, ROOTS, CANDLES, FLOWERS, AND OILS - FOLK AFRICAN SPIRITUAL TRADITIONS AND EASY AND ADVANCED MAGIC SPELLS

By Maria Butfield

OrangePen Publications is a company of writers, designers, editors,researchers and other professionals, who have formed a team to create and publish unique and extraordinary works of literature.

The main purpose of *OrangePen Publications* is to spread information and help people improve their lives thanks to in-depth, comprehensive communication, resulting from years of study and research. The publications cover many areas of life - health, psychology, investing, relationships, spirituality, and more - and each area has its own author.

Quality literature and customer satisfaction are primary aspects of our work, which is why the *OrangePen Publications* team continually seeks out new topics to provide content-rich, in-depth reading.

TABLE OF CONTENTS

INTRODUCTION

Hoodoo is a spiritual practice that was brought to the Americas by enslaved West Africans. It's a form of folk magic that revolves around spells and charms to ward off evil and attract good luck. Hoodoo is often used in tandem with another spiritual practice like Voodoo, which is its sister religion. It is used for healing, protection, luck, and other purposes. Practitioners of hoodoo are called hoodoos, hoodoo doctors, or conjure men and women.

Hoodoo, at its center, is an African American custom. It was made by subjugated individuals from different spiritual practices that they adjusted to the land they wound up in. Hoodoo is additionally known by different names summon or rootwork. Individuals who practice hoodoo work with various devices, like candles, trinkets, and, obviously, roots and herbs. Precursor reverence is especially significant. Motion pictures frequently show hoodoos as dark and harmful, yet a large portion of the work we do is worried about healing and assurance.

More specifically, Hoodoo is a set of legends, practices of "sympathetic" and not sympathetic magic, elementary kabbalah, traditional herbal cures, a successful synthesis of traditional folk magic that has its origins in Africa and its development in the enslaved African Americans of the late seventeenth century. It is difficult to assess the prevalence of such beliefs and practices, as the word Hoodoo often has wide usage ranging from elemental ceremonial magic to amulet making. Hoodoo is often associated with religion but rarely has a well-defined religious connotation.

There are no precise deities or developed theologies to which the Hoodoo believer or practitioner refers. It seems that religion, in Hoodoo is added, so to speak, by exclusion and that is to occupy that place that traditional belief fails to occupy because it is too little theoretical. On the altars of the practitioners, one can find images of Catholic saints, Buddhists, pagan divinities, figures that have more to do with superstition than with the sacred, folkloric symbols, sometimes the altar is simply a jumble of theological contradictions. Alongside Catholic saints such as St. Expedite, St. Photinus, St. Mary, and St. Anthony are images of Shiva, Kali, Buddha, and Mercury and so on.... All this, however, does not count for the mentality of the practitioner on duty, whose prayers and dedications go mainly to the spirits of the dead and the natural spirits that rarely have a specific connotation. It may seem strange, but it is not if we think about the essence of Hoodoo, that is the search for earthly advantages through magic.

Many people think that Hoodoo is a religious practice, but the truth is quite the opposite. Hoodoo isn't based on worshipping

Gods, Goddesses, or other formal deities. Instead, it is a way for people to practice folk magic using the most basic tools and ingredients. So, what relevance does Hoodoo have in today's society? Quite a lot! Humans are starting to understand just what powers lie in nature and how to use them.

Understanding why some plants and herbs can attract good luck while others form a protective shield appeals to our personal sense of well-being. This type of magic and conjuring can be carried out by anyone who wants to try it, providing you respect the power and learn how to protect yourself from harm.

This book has everything you need to know to perform the craft safely and powerfully. Learn the ancient craft of Hoodoo and see how it can change your life forever!

This is a tradition that has its source in spiritual practices from African cultures that were ravaged by the slave trade. In these cultures, we discover the source of many of the things hoodoo practitioners do, for example, divination, chanting (or reciting mantras), and channeling.

The reason for the development of hoodoo was a desire to change one's life, specifically in the face of being enslaved. It came out of a need to survive, to have autonomy.

Hoodoo magic has also influenced the Spiritualist, Manifestation and Wicca traditions, with which it has many similarities. Unlike most Western school forms of magic, Hoodoo magic has no tradition of summoning or negotiation with particular spirits.

The purpose of Hoodoo is usually to gain positive outcomes from everyday life to strengthen a link with the source of one's power and abilities. In African American practice, this source is traditionally the spirit world or the force of the universe. Hoodoo practitioners are concerned with the line between physical reality and the spirit world, whereas the spiritual world influences events in the physical world and the relationship between the spiritual world and the self.

Happy Reading.

CHAPTER 1: HISTORY AND ORIGINS

What is Hoodoo?

In simple terms, hoodoo is a magical and spiritual practice that emerged out of a need. 'Work' is an important word. You do work and find what works to achieve what you want.

Hoodoo is a practice that is about creating a change in our internal and external worlds. This is done through a series of methods that have been passed down for centuries.

This goes back to hoodoo being about a balance between physical and nonphysical worlds. When working with spirits, we approach from the perspective that we're working with the people who paved the way for us, often from hundreds and thousands of years back.

Hoodoo is not a modern concept, nor is it a blanket word for a number of activities, as pop culture often portrays it. Hoodoo is, in reality, a distinct tradition with its own set of rules and history. It has also been appropriated by a large number of individuals, resulting in a great deal of misinformation going around online.

At its heart, Hoodoo is an African American tradition. Enslaved people developed it by adapting different spiritual traditions to the land they found themselves in. Hoodoo is often referred to by other words, most notably "conjure" or "rootwork." Hoodoo practitioners use various instruments, including candles, trinkets, and, of course, roots and herbs. The worship of ancestors is especially important. Although Hollywood often portrays Hoodoo as dark and dangerous, most hoodoo practitioners' practice is focused on healing and defense.

When we engage with hoodoo, we are engaging with ancestors whose lives centered around the church, whether Christian or Catholic.

In addition to recognizing the spirit of the roots and plants, the conjurer in our example made a point to pay attention to the unseen forces within *herself*. She didn't just do the work and go back to the same thoughts and ideas about the money she had before. She could use the physical act of cleaning her space to stand in as a metaphor for a nonphysical act, cleansing her mind of poverty thinking. This is another example of how magick blends the physical and nonphysical worlds to create change in a person's life.

With all of these definitions and references to hoodoo, we can see why it may be difficult to trace a definite origin. Any Hoodoo belief or practice is closely related to African American/African culture and that of other cultures.

A closer look at the history of hoodoo will show that it grew from many different sources, some with ancient origins while others came from more recent practices. The two major sources for hoodoo would be African American folk magic and European witchcraft and folk magic.

Many rituals used in hoodoo have African roots. Hoodoo began as a part of the African system of folk medicine and magic that is based on the premise that nothing happens in the world without some spiritual cause or reason. This idea, along with many others, was brought to this country by slaves who were routinely forced to leave their homes and move from place to place, making it necessary for them to accept change as a part of their lives. Settlers also introduced herbs from Europe, which were well-suited for growing in our climate. For a number of years, hoodoo was practiced in the South by African Americans on their own, but it was not until the 1940s that it became more widespread.

In America there is an expression: "It's better to ask for forgiveness than permission." Some of the African American folk healers were adept at finding traditional solutions for many problems without seeking permission from the white man or even seeking permission from other black people. These solutions came from herbs gathered from plants and trees rather than from the white man's pharmacopeia. In this way, cures were handed down as "family recipes" and passed down through generations of families.

Hoodoo is a type of folk magic practiced by African Americans and many immigrants in Louisiana. It has roots that extend back to African traditions, although it has also been influenced by European practices (see hoodoo-conjure). Hoodoo begins as an attempt to use natural elements such as herbs, plants, roots, stones, and woods to cure illnesses and protect against evil forces.

Hoodoo has been found in various states throughout the South including Arkansas, Florida, Georgia, Louisiana, Mississippi,

North Carolina, and New Orleans. In many ways, hoodoo is similar to voodoo. The word hoodoo actually comes from the African word "voodoo" meaning "spirit." However, the emphasis in hoodoo is more on spells to improve your life, whereas voodoo tends to be more focused on spells cast out on others.

Hoodoo is based on the idea that every person has an energy force (or soul) within them and there are certain rituals you can perform to help re-balance the body. This idea comes from West African ideas about a person's soul. There is another force though which is also important in hoodoo: this force doesn't come from inside you, but from outside sources like plants and minerals, or even spirits of people who have died. Hoodoo practitioners are called rootworkers.

One of the most important parts of hoodoo is the idea that specific herbs, minerals and woods have energy in them (or spirits) that can be used to improve your life. For example, it is believed that a small piece of snakeskin can protect you from others' negative thoughts or that a bundle of herbs in your pocket will make you stronger. In order to use hoodoo for healing, rootworkers must first learn about these energies and use them wisely so they can benefit others rather than harm them. All in all, hoodoo is a system that helps us understand that there is no separation between God, nature, and humans.

People who practice hoodoo believe that there is a spirit force (or soul) within everyone we all have one, and what we do to our own spirits can affect our health and wellbeing. Hoodoo teaches its followers that certain herbs, minerals, and other elements can be used to help us achieve better health. Hoodoo also teaches its followers the importance of rituals in order to help achieve balance and protection. Hoodoo is often associated with Christianity though it has been influenced by African beliefs.

A Brief History of Hoodoo

Hoodoo has a long history in Louisiana and many other parts of the United States which have also been influenced by African culture, including parts of South Carolina and Georgia. It has roots that extend back to Cherokee, Choctaw, African, and European traditions. In the early 1800s, a priest named Rochard Brunnquell was introduced to hoodoo when he met suffragist activist Rachel Carson (1907-1964). He learned about hoodoo and was so intrigued that he performed a "hoodoo" wedding and began to study this African-influenced magic. He and other rootworkers in New Orleans began to practice hoodoo because their more traditional practices were not very popular with the community or the country as a whole. They eventually formed a rootwork tradition of their own which mixed traditional African beliefs with hoodoo from Louisiana.

Hoodoo evolved from traditional African religions brought to the New World by enslaved Africans. The slave owners taught them a new language, dressed them in new clothes, gave them new food to eat, and attempted to "reform" them. Although they were separated from the people and everything they knew, some things were too deeply woven into their very existence to be altered or changed.

Slaves in the New World came from many areas of Africa, but frightened, confused, and abused in a strange land, they sought each other's company, finding comfort there. Gradually, they became a community in which they shared their customs. The old ways of doing things that they'd brought with them were adjusted, tweaked, and manipulated to match their present circumstances.

Many aspects of Christianity were familiar to the African slaves. They already believed in one creator God, who was helped by powerful spirits to run the world, which they recognized in the Christian saints. They understood the Bible as a powerful spell book, and Hoodoo practitioners still use Bible verses in their work. In other words, Hoodoo is, historically, strongly based on Christianity. My grandmother Estelle, who taught me Hoodoo, was a devout Baptist and met many of her clients after church on Sunday. We don't see Hoodoo as a separate religion or as being in any way in conflict with Christianity.

The African religions evolved differently depending on where the slaves landed in the New World. For instance, in the larger Catholic plantations of Cuba, the slave owners had less direct control over the slaves, so they were better able to maintain their traditional practices. Those slaves focused more on the Catholic saints as being aspects of spirits from their homeland, and their practices grew into Santeria. In Haiti, also strongly Catholic, the practices grew into Voodoo, which played a large part in the revolution that freed the island's slaves from the French. In other places, the African religions developed into practices like Candomblé, which was practiced in Brazil.

Hoodoo Today

Today, spiritual supplies' stores and traditional practitioners continue to operate, despite Hoodoo's evolution. Recent intellectual developments have contributed significantly to the transformation of conjure from a taboo element of African American life to a widely accepted model of supernaturalism open to all. The emergence of postmodernism among artists and intellectuals has aided in the dismantling of long-held beliefs about Hoodoo. The heart of postmodern thought is that all moral authority is subjective and can only be determined by one's actions. Along with increasing respect for African American heritage, this way of thinking has greatly increased exposure to the role of supernaturalism and creole religions in black life. This new perspective is reflected in a growing number of artworks and literary works dedicated to them. Similarly, many African American women regarding conjure to reconnect with their African ancestors and a long history of strong female hoodoo practitioners. Hoodoo can no longer be simply described as devilish by those who opposed it, at least not without disagreement.

Although the implications of postmodernism are readily evident to theorists and other users of high culture, they are not so visible to the majority of practitioners and believers. They also put a much higher premium on the New Age and Neopagan movements. Indeed, the closely linked movements can be viewed as popular culture's response to postmodernism. Notably, both postmodernists and New Agers/Neopagans disregard conventional sources of authority, favoring personal knowledge and conviction. Neopagans and New Age followers, the majority of whom are wealthy whites, choose to construct personal collages of values from various cultures and peoples rather than embracing Christianity or whatever else is considered normative by their heritage.

Since the first African slaves carried their ancient practices to the New World, conjure, Hoodoo, and Voodoo have evolved dramatically. In the United States, an ancient African creole religion has not been commonly practiced since the early twentieth century. In addition, traditional practitioners who collect magical resources from nature are becoming increasingly scarce. The fact that modern conjurers are almost as likely to be white as they are black would have astounded nineteenth-century observers beyond words. Unsurprisingly, a legacy of such change would foster discussion among artists, writers, academics, and the general public.

Many of our everyday practices can have magical uses. Take a shower, organize your files and workspace, cook, work exercise and even use the bathroom. Anything and everything can have a hoodoo application if you're willing to get creative and open your mind.

You could say hoodoo is everywhere. A basic concept in hoodoo is paying respect to the things we can and cannot see. It is a way to connect, work with, and respect the powerful natural forces and world around us and the forces that remain unseen to the naked eye.

By natural forces, I mean the earth: plants, trees, herbs, and dirt. More specifically, actual roots from plants, trees, and herbs. Common roots you will hear of are High John the Conqueror, Mandrake, Licorice, and Angelica.

Unseen forces are exactly that: unseen. The air is often mentioned as an example of a force that we can't see, but one we know exists. The same could be said of WIFI.

When it comes to hoodoo, we're talking about forces that are a little easier to deny. What our ancestors knew was (and is) that the spirit world is just as "real" as our 3D world. Colonizers saw how they lived, how close they were to Spirit, and immediately labeled it as evil.

Unfortunately, this mindset spread and eventually, it wasn't the colonizer saying working with spirits was 'evil'; it was the descendants of our ancestors.

You may have encountered people who think like this in your life. If you want to build your practice, you have to give yourself permission to see things differently.

Hoodoo Beliefs

Let's talk about exactly what Hoodoo is in practical terms. It shares many qualities with practices like Voodoo and European-based witchcraft, so it's important to know what is different about Hoodoo.

Ancestral Veneration

I think working with the spirits of our ancestors is, perhaps, the key part of Hoodoo that separates it from other spiritual and magical practices. The spirits of your ancestors can be called on for aid and guidance. It's important to develop a relationship with your ancestors and not simply call on them when you're in need, like a fair-weather friend who you only hear from when they need something from you.

Rootwork

There is power in roots and herbs, and you can call on that power. In Hoodoo, we call this rootwork, and you'll find roots and herbs in nearly every Hoodoo spell. You can usually understand why an herb is used by understanding the plant it came from, the aspects of the herb itself, or its effects on the human body. For instance, cinnamon is a common herb used to speed up drawing work because cinnamon is both sweet and a bit warm to the tongue. The sweetness will draw things to it, just like a bear being drawn to honey. And the heat will make the work faster, just like in cooking or chemistry.

The Power of the Earth

There are two special cases of using earth that I want to discuss in a bit more detail, and the first is graveyard dirt. Graveyard dirt is special because it can be used in many different ways and because collecting it is more involved than it is at other locations. Dirt in a graveyard hasn't just collected the energy of a place, it has also collected the energy of the spirits that reside in that graveyard. A graveyard is home to many spirits, like a neighborhood, and you should not enter such a place without showing respect. First, whenever you enter a graveyard, you should cover your head. This is both a sign of respect and a way to block the spirits from attaching themselves to your mind. Second, always bring with you an offering to leave at the entrance. This can take several forms, but the most common are rum, sweet bread, or three pennies.

Who Can Practice Hoodoo?

Remember this—rootwork is not a religion. It is a practice that is inherited solely by birth line. You are born into being able to practice hoodoo. You are born into a line of family members that likely has some sort of history with hoodoo. In particular, if you have no descendants of Africans enslaved in the United States, you lack the spiritual connection that you would need. Without that spiritual connection, how can you call upon your ancestors? Though some recipes may claim that they have a European influence, remember that the Europeans segregated the enslaved Africans—they were kept entirely separate and therefore did not socialize. Those recipes that claim that they have European influence are a dead giveaway that they are not actually authentic Hoodoo recipes.

Hoodoo Principles

Respect for Ancestors

Who are we working with when we practice? Who are the spirits that help us on the other side? Who helps us in ways we can't see or recognize?

You might not know who your ancestors are by name, but they know who you are. Reverence to those who have worked hard so we can live the way we live is a core principle of hoodoo practice.

It took some time for me to listen to my ancestors' voices and be confident that they were with me in the first place. I'm guessing that you weren't raised in a home where it was common to talk to ancestors, and if my guess is correct, then you and I have this in common.

Respect for Environment

Hoodoo is a practice that looks different, depending on which region you are in. New Orleans is probably the most notable example of this. You might not have a hoodoo practice specific to where you live, but what I want you to take from this is you and your environment come first.

You might find a working online that asks for Angelica root, but if this is hard to find in your region, this is something you need to be aware of, at least. Most of us are lucky to live in countries where anything we want is accessible if we're willing to pay for the shipping.

You'll also want to be mindful of going out and picking fresh flowers and plants. This is knowing what plants grow natively in your region, what trees and plants are endangered and which ones thrive. This might require getting another book to research botanicals, but if you're serious about this practice, then you don't need much convincing.

Hearing the Ego

The more you learn to listen to the voice of your own ego, the more you'll hear it speak to you in patterns. One common pattern that all of us know is statements around an idea that sounds like "I'm not good enough." Thinking someone else is "better" than you at something, like talking to spirit, is an example of this type of thinking.

The benevolent ancestors you call on can help with hearing their voice over your own as well. Again, the only thing you need to do is ask. If it sounds like I'm talking about capital-s Spirit, that is on purpose. Your benevolent ancestors are connected with Spirit, with Infinite Love, Infinite Abundance, and Infinite Wisdom.

It's this connection that will help you live in balance and maintain that balance in your hoodoo and conjure work.

Another mindset that we're quick to shift to, especially as we consider solving our problems with magic, is that we are stupid for having the problems we have in the first place, that the

Differences between Hoodoo and Voodoo

Hoodoo is NOT Voodoo (Vodou). Hoodoo is the folk magic of the southern United States devoid of any religious connection. It is a magical technology - pure and simple - developed by the black descendants of African slaves brought to this country. As has already been mentioned, most Hoodoo practitioners are Protestant Christians.

Voodoo, more correctly spelled Vodou, is a separate and distinct religion originating from the island of Haiti. It is one of the African diasporic faiths that evolved in the Caribbean as a result of the destructive legacy of the slave trade. African tribes that never had any dealings or even knew about each other were forced to live and work jointly. In an attempt to safeguard their native religions, they merged many of their beliefs into a conglomerate practice. The Vodou was the result. Vodou practitioners worship God and Jesus primarily through the recitation of French Catholic prayers and through the Catholic mass, but they also worship and operate with their native African spirits and powers, known as lwa or loa. Vodou is an initiatory religion where specialists dedicate their life and ritual to the lwa through religious consecration. Vodou is not a malevolent religion as many portray it to be. It is a charming religion that has preserved the native religious practices of the African citizens who endured terrible pain at the hands of slave owners. It should be respected and honored, but it is not Hoodoo or Rootwork.

Hoodoo is a voodoo style of magic that focuses on the supernatural and the practical use of spells. In reality, it's a combination of many magical traditions that focus on spiritualism, mysticism, and craft. Hoodoo magic differs from Voodoo in that it's a widespread practice in the south and works more like alchemy than a religion.

There are many important differences between hoodoo and Voodoo. The key difference is that hoodoo is typically Christian in nature, while Voodoo is not. This means that Christian practitioners usually cast hoodoo spells. You'll notice that most hoodoo magic spells are intended to take care of problems or help someone with their life.

Many people confuse hoodoo with Vodou, which is a religion and magic system practiced primarily in Haiti. Vodou and hoodoo's main difference is that Vodou is an entire religion devoted to honoring and communicating with spirits. Hoodoo tends to be more of a practical magic system focused on solving problems instead of gaining mystical knowledge about the world around us.

Hoodoo is a form of Voodoo that emerged in the American South after the Civil War. Hoodoo magic stems from African traditions, and both forms are distinctive in their focus on herbs and other plant materials. However, it is important to note that hoodoo magic differs from its southern counterpart in its magical approach.

There are many essential differences between hoodoo and voodoo magic. First of all, voodoo magic focuses on the transference of energy from one living thing to another, whereas hoodoo magic relies on herbal remedies to heal ailments or cure diseases. Voodoo uses its language, a phraseology rooted in West African languages, while hoodoo magic is generally easier to understand as it uses English phrases to convey its magical intentions. The use of herbs in hoodoo is also highly regulated and controlled.

Hoodoo remedies were originally used by poor southerners who lacked medical care for various illnesses or diseases. In some cases, herbs were used instead of traditional medicines or treatments because they had known curative properties to replace the medics.

Voodoo, as opposed to hoodoo, is a type of magic practiced by its practitioners (called voodooists) and is often associated with the religion of the same name. This folk culture practice is made up of a mix of African beliefs in witchcraft and magic that came from there and European Catholic traditions. Voodoo practitioners have "god-mother" figures in their religion like houngans and mambos (male and female priests). These high priests do not have the same kind of power that Christian priests have. They act more like community leaders than holy men or women. Many voodooists believe that they are in touch with the "spirit world" and get messages from their ancestors through dreams, visions or other mediums. Many voodooists also perform animal sacrifices and carry on traditional funerals similar to those done for the dead.

Voodoo is practiced by people of African descent, although it has spread beyond this group to other people of African descent as well as to others of Caribbean descent. The religion of voodoo is very different though. Many African Americans have turned to voodoo because they are frustrated with hoodoo and don't want to follow its more "legendary" elements.

The term Voodoo comes from the name of a small island, apparently a by-word for witchcraft in the Caribbean. The word is believed to mean "don't wake up," also in reference to the fact that people said they would be punished if they performed harmful magic rites while their minds were still asleep. Some say voodoo was an abomination brought by the French along with other slaves, while others say it was an ancient African religious cult that was brought to Haiti along with other aspects of West African culture such as stories and legends.

Local legends say that voodoo practitioners worked with the devil, made deals with the dead and participated in voodoo rites. So if you heard someone talk about "voodoo," they were most likely referring to hoodoo. The term Voodoo has been used to describe any aspect of West African culture since the early 19th century.

Hoodoo is American, Vodou is Haitian. Hoodoo is a magical tradition without religious attachment, while Vodou is a religion. Hoodoo is an assortment of spells and magical techniques that any individual can perform, while Vodou is an initiatory and community-based religion. Hoodoo practitioners make use of roots, herbs and minerals to create preparations or spells for their customers, empowered in the name of the Christian God, while Vodou introduces work with the lwa through divine insight and intercession to help or introduce others. As well-intentioned as these people may be, mixing Hoodoo and Vodou is not only disrespectful to both practices, it confuses most people and muddies the spiritual waters.

Hoodoo Books

First, we will talk about the book most used by Conjure men: the bible.

The bible is considered by many Conjure men as "the greatest of magical books." Besides using the invocations and the passages of the bible (especially of the Old Testament) as magic formulas, the Conjure man has very peculiar concepts of interpretation of the passages and principles of the bible. The most used passages are certainly the psalms; there are 150 of them and to each one, the root doctor associates a specific efficacy in the field of magic. There are psalms to make good journeys, psalms of protection, psalms of consecration, psalms to ward off the enemy or to strike him, psalms effective in matters of love, gambling and so on. They are so used that some modern Conjure man has written specific treatizes on the subject, for example, the famous "power of the psalms" by Godfrey Selig. The bible is therefore considered a 'huge treaty of Hoodoo. God is considered the greatest of root doctors and the creation of the universe is interpreted as a grandiose work of magic.

People have the right to practice Hoodoo and magic because God gives man all of creation and the ability to name (and therefore command) all creatures. Moreover, since God punishes, blesses, helps or curses and he knows and foresees everything, why shouldn't this punishment or blessing pass through the hands of the Conjure man, making him a divine instrument? Moses is considered a great Conjure man and is attributed to him even two apocryphal books used by rootworkers, the sixth and seventh book of Moses (actually two grimoires probably renaissance). How to explain then the prohibition of magic in the Mosaic Law? Simple: Moses was forbidden to the common people the practice of Hoodoo, to reserve it to the class of priests. In fact it may seem strange, but these explanations and interpretations are supported by biblical citations. We can give some examples, also reported by the famous Rootworker Doctor Kioni, regarding stories of "biblical Hoodoo":

- In Genesis 30: 1,43 Jacob makes the white sheep drink by putting stripped and worked sticks in the water so that the sheep give birth to ragged instead of white children;

- In the first book of Samuel 30:7,20, King David asks God for a response, and God responds through the stones of the priest's breastplate (today we would say a work of divination);

- In the book of Numbers 5: 11,31 it is said that to find out if a wife has cheated one can go to the priest, who will make her drink water consecrated with powder taken from the tabernacle, and will curse the water so that if the woman has cheated, she will also be cursed.

These are not the only examples that can be given, in fact, the bible is full of these "authorized Hoodoo works" despite being prohibited by Mosaic Law. On the other hand, the boundary between magic ritual and religious ritual is often blurred; beyond the meanings and authorizations, the magician considers himself a priest and acts accordingly.

We can say that perhaps the interpretation of the root doctor is dictated by convenience, but not without support in the text.

Other books widely used by the Hoodoo man are the already mentioned sixth and seventh book of Moses, two grimoires of vague biblical inspiration that are nothing more than catalogs of formulas and magic diagrams of ready use inspired by the actions of Moses, interpreted as acts of Hoodoo. Thus we will find the formulas with which Moses defeated the Egyptian magicians in the well-known episode, with which he made the plague of hail come down, and even a couple of formulas that say to make God appear in person in front of whoever pronounces them (!). Finally, another text is the grimoire called "pow-wow or the long lost friend." It's a set of spells and formulas of surely central European origin imported at the end of 800 by the Dutch community emigrated to America. In it, there are formulas that should solve common evils (worms, bruises, wounds) as well as spells against evil, bad spirits, and bad luck. Actually, the Conjure man often does not use the formulas for the actions stated in the books, but he uses them, adapting them to his own case, exactly as he does for the psalms.

The formula of Moses against the Egyptian magicians could be used to win an enemy, the one for hail to destroy it, the one for the divine apparition to bless herbs and preparations. Once again, we find in practice great freedom even if assisted by principles of operation that are fundamentally traditional. Even in some cases, the book acts as a real amulet (pow-wows also have this function) or is used per se to ward off bad spirits (for example, the bible is left open to a certain page on the altar, directing it in a certain direction). There are many other books and books that can be used in the practice of Hoodoo, to examine them one by one would go beyond the scope of this article, as well as being virtually impossible. Consider only the fact that in addition to traditional, regional, imported books, there are also books written from scratch by today's Conjure men.

Difference between Wicca and Hoodoo- 21 Voodoo Divisions

First and most importantly, modern witchcraft is NOT used to communicate with the devil! This is an example of how the folklore and superstitions of the past have bled into the present and continue to color the practice today.

In a general sense, witchcraft *should* be defined as behaviors that fall under the casting of spells that either have a positive or negative effect on the individual who is the focal point of the spell. Yes, witchcraft can be used to have negative effects on people; referred to as "black magick." However, we will be staying on the positive, affirming, "white magick" side of witchcraft. Witchcraft should be an act that promotes self-awareness, healing, and all-around the well-being of an individual.

The beautiful part of witchcraft is that it is completely driven by YOU! There is no liturgical or holy book, there are no services to attend every week, and there are no donation plates to pass around. Your witchcraft practice is dependent on your own intent on your time. The world is your sanctuary.

Wicca is the "religion" of witchcraft. So, if you ask ten Wiccans their spiritual beliefs, you are likely to get ten different answers. However, there are some core principles and beliefs which are common to the vast majority of modern Wiccan sects. Let's explore some of these overarching beliefs.

Wicca acknowledges the *duality* of the divine, meaning that both the male and female aspects of divinity - a God and a Goddess. Depending upon the tradition that the Wiccan ascribes to, the God and Goddess can be known by many different names: Isis and Osiris, Cerridwen and Herne, Apollo and Athena, *etc.* There are even traditions that honor a non-gender specific deity (still encompassing both the male and female aspects, but not identified as "male" and "female"). In many Gardnerian sects, the names of the honored deities are revealed only to initiated members and kept secret from all people outside of their sect.

The belief in and use of *magick* is nearly a universal principle among Wiccans. Magick is viewed within Wicca as the redirection of natural forces through manipulation on the spirit plane to realize or manifest the practitioner's intent. This is where evil can become a problem within Wicca. There are spells (curses) that can be used to cause injury or negativity to occur to another individual. In order to perform that type of magick (black magic), the intent of the practitioner must be evil. The intent of the practitioner is extremely important to spell work. Magick can be used for good or magick can be used for evil, and oftentimes, the difference is found in the heart (the intent) of the practitioner.

Each person has the right and, indeed, the responsibility to choose their own spiritual path. Quite frankly, Wicca is not for everyone. If the beliefs and principles of Wicca do not fall in line with your personal beliefs, find a different path. It is important for the conviction of the Wiccan that they search out Wicca, not have Wicca thrust upon them, nor should they expect everyone around them to convert to Wicca. Although we do not necessarily receive the same from other organized religions, Wiccans are to fully respect the spiritual beliefs of others.

21 Divisions

There are, first and foremost, several traditions of voodoo. Although they share a common matrix, Africa, and similarities, they are, in reality, very different in their myths, rituals, practices, metaphysical conceptions and spirits. Even the way entities are conceived varies from one place to another. It is a bit like talking about Christianity, we find Roman Catholicism, Protestant Christianity, the evangelical sects... all have the figure of Jesus Christ in common, but each interprets it differently because of enlightened personalities who founded a "new" religiosity, or because of political motivations that pushed a particular Church, as in the case of the Anglican Church at the time of Henry VIII, to break away from the mother church of Rome.

The African voodoo of the origins is still practiced in Africa, in Togo and Benin, but it is profoundly different from the various types of voodoo we find in the diaspora.

Haitian voodoo is certainly the best known. It is called 21 nachons (21 nations) because the divinities are considered according to their original place of origin in specific ways. It revolves around the structure of the hounfor (temple), each of which is governed by a priest or a priestess (houngan and mambo). It is extremely complex in ritualistic and elaborate in practices. One arrives at the priesthood only after many sacrifices, physical and economical, and it takes years to complete the initiation cycle that characterizes it.

The voodoo of New Orleans derives from the Haitian one and has a deeply magical mark. In relation to the Haitian one, it is simplified, less divinities are considered, and the ritualistic is less complex and structured.

The voodoo of Puerto Rico is called Sanse, and it is a kind of Umbanda spiritism associated with the lwà, while the Dominican voodoo, the one we will deal with in this text, is distinguished by the strong recourse to syncretism and for the modalities of the cult.

If it is true that in part it is of Haitian derivation, it is also true that Dominican voodoo is not only Haitian, but has its own history and its own path and is legitimized by nothing less than a group of lwà (spirits) who have the task of protecting the purity of this extraordinary tradition. In Dominican voodoo, there is no honor (temple), but rather there are centers in which the initiates perform ceremonies; there is no strict dependence between initiate and initiator. Who is "baptized" is considered free and does not depend on anyone; there is no assòn (the ritual rattle of the Haitian tradition to call the spirits); there are no blood sacrifices (if not in very rare cases); everyone, regardless of whether they are initiated or not, can serve the lwà and get any kind of help from the divinities; even an uninitiated person can be "caballo del santo" (literally, "horse of the saint"), that is to say, a horse of the saint. Even an uninitiated person can be "caballo del santo" (literally, "horse of the saint"), i.e., be possessed by a lwa; it is evident that whoever is endowed with this gift will normally have an incentive to receive initiation and baptism in the tradition. The priests of Dominican voodoo are called papabokòs if men and mambosas if females. Dominican voodoo tends to be softer and less aggressive than Haitian voodoo and not all lwà correspond in both traditions. The myths related to the deities are different. If Haitian voodoo has 21 nations, Dominican voodoo is called 21 divisions or Dominican Santeria. In fact, the entities are considered not by reason of origin but by reason of vibration and mode of implementation.

To each lwà, the supreme spirit of voodoo corresponds a Catholic saint. Dominican syncretism is not necessarily the same as Haitian syncretism even if there are many similarities.

Dominican voodoo operates in most cases for positive purposes. The faithful ask the lwà for well-being, health, protection, defense, money and advancement in life. If it's true that there are attack practices, it's also true that very rarely lwà are used, even the most aggressive ones, to do evil for pure pleasure. The entities are mainly used to solve the problems of everyday life. While it is true that there are individuals who use these powers incorrectly, it is also true that such behavior is neither encouraged nor approved.

<u>**Oration at 21 Divisions**</u>

This prayer is recited to impart special graces to the 21 Divisions, but also as an opening prayer in rituals of this tradition.

Light a seven-day candle of seven colors in front of an image of the 21 Divisions; place a glass with water on the side. Begin the prayer on a Monday or Friday.

I invoke the sublime influence of the 21 Divisions to achieve good success and progress in every area of my life and to smooth out all the difficulties I may encounter on my path. I invoke the help of the Holy Spirit so that the stars illuminate my path and drive away any evil shadow that may follow me. I invoke the God of Heights that my home may prosper, my business may increase, and my person may receive a message of good fortune from Divine Providence.

Oh, Great Power of God, I implore your powerful help to keep me out of danger at the right time and to illuminate my path with the beacon of good fortune. I will receive the infinite blessings of heaven, I believe in God the Father Almighty. Amen. (Our Father and Hail Mary).

CHAPTER 2: GETTING STARTED WITH HOODOO

Where to Start For Beginners?

Hoodoo practitioners believed in a number of spirits, including cleansing and protective ones, such as saint-like imagery and animals like owls and ravens. Other spirits included those associated with disease or death, such as ghosts, zombies, or evil spirits like witches.

Hoodoo practitioners worked with these powers in many ways. Spells and charms were used to bring about change in a person's life, much as they are used by many people today for the same purpose.

Spells were also used to bring good luck, protect oneself from spells cast by others, and ensure that one's wishes were granted. Practitioners of hoodoo usually gathered herbs from their backyards for use in spells or for healing purposes. These herbs were believed to have special powers and could be used in combination with other ingredients that were thought to provide the desired results.

Hoodoo practitioners were very careful not to harm themselves through their practices. Hoodoo spells and charms often contained a warning not to use them for ill purposes against anyone else, or they could come back on you three times as hard in the form of bad luck or evil magic.

The traditional language of hoodoo, also called conjure talk, was usually English. However, some practitioners may have used African languages such as Yoruba or Fon to perform deeper hoodoo magic. The term hoodoo is itself a Southern African American language word that means "bad luck" or "jinx.

Hoodoo Practitioners

Many of the women who practiced hoodoo did so because they were not allowed to learn more "common" forms of magic and witchcraft. As a result, most people who practiced this type of magic were considered outsiders by mainstream society. The practitioners were often called upon to help with issues that mainstream society was either too afraid or too unwilling to deal with on their own. Many times, these issues involved either the presence or destruction of evil influences. The practitioner could then use hoodoo to help rid the space of these influences and restore it to a more desirable state.

Women also used this practice for personal healing or even in beauty rituals. The African American women who practiced hoodoo were not just concerned with their own health, but also with that of others in their community. Hoodoo spells and charms were often used as a method of protection from bad luck, harm, or misfortune. Women would seek out the help of other women who had knowledge or experience through this practice to seek help with the issues they faced in their own lives.

African American men also sought out hoodoo practitioners for various reasons as well. They often sought out hoodoo practitioners to help with issues involving their families. Some of the most common reasons were to get rid of unkind spirits, ghosts, or harmful influences in their homes in which they were unable to do so otherwise themselves.

Many traditional African American styles of religious practices such as hoodoo were passed on down through history and across generations until they finally disappeared into other cultures and are now a part of a whole new group of traditions. However, the practice is still alive today within African

American communities. It is a blend of African culture, European tradition, and Native American spirituality.

In the past, many people believed that magic was something that only certain people could perform. They believed that the practice of hoodoo was a way for these special people to harness the power of their magical practices. While today's beliefs may be different, we can still utilize hoodoo in order to better deal with the issues and challenges we face in our own lives. As long as we stay true to ourselves and good spirits will help us along the way.

How to Practice Hoodoo

Dipping your toes into the hoodoo can seem daunting. With no familiarity with what it is and how it works, just finding a spell for you can be a challenge, especially when you are new to the practice.

If you have to work in secret from nosy friends and family, getting a package of 7-day candles, Florida water, and holy oils might not be so easy.

And that's not to mention the costs. There are the costs of buying what you need for a working and possibly the costs of setting up an altar.

As with everything, part of respecting your ancestors, your environment, and yourself means doing your research and knowing what works for you. Copying spells from someone else is fine, but with your knowledge and knowing the core elements of hoodoo, you are better equipped to create your own workings.

If you know the core elements of hoodoo, this becomes easier with time. This is where we incorporate many of the topics we've covered already. In hoodoo, the spirit is at the core of everything. Practitioners think about the spirit of everything they work with, what is at the core or root.

As mentioned, hoodoo exists to make your life easier. Do not burden yourself with getting supplies and materials that someone else says you need for a spell.

There is a way to practice with what's readily available to you. The things you already touch and experience every day can be used in your hoodoo. Plus, you probably already have some powerful herbs in your kitchen cabinets. Often items you have just hanging around as decor, like candles and seashells, can be used in your work.

Working with Spirit

Your day might start with a prayer acknowledging the ancestors and reconnecting with the work you're doing in your life. A practice could begin with acknowledging those who went before you and the power they lend to you.

If you don't have an image or any idea of who your ancestors are, this might seem like a challenge. This is one of the painful consequences of the slave trade; many descendants of ancestors living in North America don't have any connection to those who came before them.

Many of my clients know this pain intimately. Some of them come from families who just do not seem to care about their lineage, so their questions and quest for knowledge are met with indifference, if not anger.

Their blood still runs through your veins, and in this way, you will stay connected to them for as long as you are alive.

Working with Nature

The term 'rootwork' is interchangeable with hoodoo. Other than roots, natural elements, such as herbs, plants, seeds, leaves, peels, and dirt, play an important role in hoodoo practice. Take any vegetable or plant you have or that grows around you.

An orange can feed your body, but the peel can also be used in working for luck and money. Same with fennel seeds and bay leaves.

Each of the natural powers we use in hoodoo pulled their power in from the earth. Not only does the earth power the growth of the plants and herbs you use, but it also powers our own growth.

It feeds us every day and grounds us in place, even as we run around and get distracted with living life.

Often, we get so enthusiastic about a spell we're looking around to find a store that sells everything in one place. Before buying roots and herbs was a possibility, conjurers either grew what they used on their own, or got what they needed straight from the source: the earth.

If you can, try to forage what you need or grow it on your own. This might mean doing a few substitutions here and there, and if you choose to use an alternate ingredient, be careful to understand what results you might get with what you're using.

Working with Waters

I'm using 'waters' here as a metaphor for cleansing and purification. Your energy is affected by countless things on any given day. Our world continuously bombards us with all types of ideas that can either zap our energy or empower us.

Let's be honest, we're more likely to be drawn to the things that zap our energy.

Need I list examples? The news, social media, gossip, YouTube channels, reality television, trauma fiction. Going out and having a negative interaction with someone on the street or in a grocery store is a prime example of the kind of interaction that can muck up your energy.

Of course, we'd all like to think we're immune to the energy of others, but even with a strong mental and vibrational shield, most people need to continuously keep their field maintained.

In this way, your spirit is a lot like your physical body. It requires work to keep healthy and in tune. As sensitive people, we are open to absorbing negative energies that need to be removed regularly.

We'll talk more about cleansing in another section, but for now, know that within hoodoo there are various liquids; oils, colognes, perfumes, spiritual waters, and vinegars that are used for multiple purposes. There are money drawing oils, two types of Florida Water, war and peace water, and Four Thieves Vinegar, for example.

Working with Place

Graveyards and crossroads are two important places in hoodoo because of the energy they carry. Other places that you'll often hear or read about in your research are banks and churches.

Specifically, you'll most often work with the spirit of a place like a bank by using the dirt from the land around where it is located (if it's surrounded by concrete, that is another story). You could really get creative with this, but using dirt from just anywhere could produce unintended results.

The symbolism of crossroads is also big in conjure. The crossroads represent many things. In our plane of existence, we live in a world where we can experience both 3D life and the spirit world.

Hoodoo as a Way of Life

You can't talk about Hoodoo from a native perspective without going into stories from the motherland. These stories were orally passed on to us by our ancestors. You will not find them on the pages of history books. Even in the books of those who have tried to chronicle our history for us, Hoodoo is not a religion or a belief. It is the way we live our lives.

Our ancestors lived off the land. This meant that when they were sick, it was the land that provided healing. If they needed love, they turned to the land. On the land is where they would find water, herbs, and any other accouterments that, when combined, could provide solutions to the problems that plagued them. Courage, community, and culture inspired them at every level and continue to inspire us.

What do I mean by courage, you may wonder? Courage to face problems head-on instead of running away from them. Courage to embrace every part of oneself even though it may not favorably tally up against the opinions of the public. Courage to do what is necessary to achieve the results you desire. This was the kind of courage my people spoke and sang about.

When it comes to community, our practice is a communal one. The energy that we tap into when creating spells is a powerful communal or ancestral energy. We feed on the energy of our past and bind it to our will/intention in the present.

Finally, we come to culture, which is our way of life. Hoodoo is not some secret cult practice that we hide in the back of our closet only to put on a mask to present when we are in public. It is the very essence of who we are. The more you incorporate Hoodoo into your day-to-day living, the more powerful your spells will become.

When you create spells after Hoodoo has already become a part of you, those spells will be more potent.

Your Ancestor Altar

One of the most sacred aspects of Hoodoo practice is the space where you carry out your spell. Within our community, this space is commonly known as the ancestral altar. This is where you pay homage to the ancestors who paved the way for you and then tap into their powers to create and manifest the desires of your heart. An altar is a place of transformation and the starting point of manifestation.

The altar is the space through which your ancestors can give their blessings and pour their power into the spells cast by you. It is where you will feel the most powerful. Your altar is crucial to your Hoodoo practice and is traditionally meant to be somewhere in your home. However, it is not uncommon to place it outside your home, in a location where you feel most connected to your ancestors.

CHAPTER 3: CLEANSING

Before doing any Hoodoo, it's important to perform some kind of spiritual cleansing. Having a regular cleanse is the way of life for people who practice Hoodoo. For us, a cleanse is beyond washing off your body with soap and water. You have to purify yourself and this purification provides fortification.

When you tamper with powers beyond the physical plane, you expose yourself. With or without fortification, there are dark spirits that will ride on the waves of that ancestral connection and enter into your space. A thorough cleanse will ward off their impact and cause them to be powerless. But when you fail to do a cleanse, you will absorb that impact, and as you continue to cast spells, they will begin to change form and become darker until the darkness consumes you. If the spell is intended to be a love spell, this darkness will also consume the person your spell is directed at.

Spiritual Cleansing

Spiritual cleansing in the American South is often done through a technique called Hoodoo. While this tradition does not always use what one may classify as "magic," it does employ methods that many would define as superstitious.

This practice is used to ward off evil spirits and to provide the practitioner with good luck. A practitioner of Hoodoo might also perform other rituals such as palm reading and using amulets in an effort to attract or maintain the favor of an individual or group. In addition, Hoodoos will often resort to performing elaborate ceremonies in order to achieve goals such as finding a new job or improving a relationship.

Hoodoo talismans are believed to protect the wearer from evil spirits, negative energies or bad luck. These items are either handmade by hoodoo practitioners themselves or purchased in a store. Many times hoodoo practitioners will make their own mixture of herbs and roots to use in the creation of their magical talisman.

A gris-gris or mojo bag is a small cloth bag filled with herbs, roots and other materials. These items are worn close to the body in order to carry one's intent or goal. This item can be sewn by hand or purchased at a store.

A conjure doll is a very powerful magical object that is created for the purpose of attracting a specific person into one's life. Conjure dolls are usually dressed in clothing that represents the person they are intended for. However, these dolls are also filled with personal items of the individual they are made for as well as herbs and other magical ingredients that supposedly attract that particular person to come into one's life.

Hoodoo practitioners also use candles made from beeswax or tallow (animal fat). These candles are used for a variety of spells, such as love, luck, protection, and to increase one's income. This candle magic is very popular with many practitioners of hoodoo that desire financial stability.

Most African-based spiritual traditions use a mixture of charms and talismans to protect the home and family. Hoodoo practitioners use similar methods to connect with their deities in order to help them achieve their goals in life. Hoodoo is also known as Conjure, Rootwork or Faith Healing.

Personal Cleansing

This form of ritual is especially important if you are feeling under the weather or anxious about something. If you feel like your powers are waning and you have blockages in your aura, then cleansing your body and soul will help you restore your energy levels.

Cleansing is one of the most important parts of conjure work, and it's essential to make time for your rituals. To get the best results to perform the cleansing during certain planetary hours. This will increase the powers of your ritual and give them added intentions. Use an online planetary hour calculator to calculate the body that rules the day and choose the best day for you.

Now take a jug and pour the water over your head 13 times while reciting a cleansing prayer. Psalm 37 is a prayer option, or you can compose your own prayer. Only wash downward, so negative energies are flushed into the bathwater. Once you feel refreshed and cleansed, step out of the bath and air dry yourself (no drying with towels) before dressing in clean clothes. Now take a jug full of the bathwater before draining the rest. Take your saved bathwater and head for a crossroads. Throw the water over your shoulder and then walk back home without looking back. If you are lucky enough to have trees in your garden, you can dispose of the bathwater by throwing it at the trunk so it can absorb the negativity.

Handy tip: This type of bath can be used as an attraction bath with a few simple changes. Use the same ingredients but add rose petals or other floral essential oils to your water. Wash in an upward manner and pour the water over your head 7 or 9 times. Recite Psalm 23 or other uplifting text while you wash and then air dry yourself before dressing. Using yellow or red candles will make the object of your attraction more attainable, and the saved water should be used to wash your front doorstep and be swept inwards to bring the attraction toward you.

<u>Quick-Fix Methods of Cleansing Yourself</u>

If you can't use baths to cleanse yourself because you don't have the time or just need a quick fix, you can use several following methods to remove negativity.

- **The chicken foot:** This is a wonderful tool for cleansing, and lightly scratching yourself with it will keep your energy positive and will remove any negative energies. Think how the chicken deals with its mess. It simply scratches it away and moves on!

- **Brushing:** If you feel like your cleansing should be more rigorous, but you want to use natural elements, then upgrade to a turkey or chicken wing. If you feel the need to remove a crossing or a jinx, take the turkey wing and brush it down from the top of your head to the base of your feet. Traditionally turkeys gobble up all the mess, so the wing will remove the condition and cleanse your aura.

- **Rubdown:** Use your alcohol rub to form a base. Add herbs and oils to infuse the mixture before rubbing yourself down. Perform the ritual in a sacred place and use prayers and spiritual chants to enhance the experience.

- **Candle Cleansing:** Use a black candle to remove a crossed or jinxed condition. Wipe yourself with the candle in downward movements while praying.

- **Smoke Cleansing:** Also known as smudging, this process can be performed by burning incense, essential oils, or dried herbs. Use a white cloth to cover yourself from the neck down and burn the selected items under it. Allow the smoke to swirl around you before removing the sheet and allowing the smoke to permeate the house.

- **Sprinkle:** Use a sprinkler head to perform this ritual. Fill it with holy or blessed water and add salt and essential oils to the liquid. Sprinkle your head and shoulders with the water, recite your favorite psalm (psalm 23 works well), and then sprinkle your feet.

Cleansing and Blessing the Home

Floor washes based on the elements used in cleansing baths can be used to clean houses and other physical places. The same rule of directing energies applies to floor washes, just like it applies to bathing. Wash windows and doors downward to dispel negativity and upward to attract goods, luck, and wealth. Candles, prayers, and smudging can all be used to give your cleanse added depth.

Hoodoo practitioners will often use elemental ingredients to increase the power of their house cleanses and blessings. Here are a few ways to use these strong influences in your rituals: *Earth* Actual dirt is the most basic elemental form of Earth, but not everyone wants to have dirt on their floor. Several substitutes can be used just as effectively.

- **Redbrick dust:** Hoodoo practitioners believe this form of Earth is particularly effective, and they will sprinkle it almost everywhere. Doorways and windows, thresholds, and entrances should all be protected, and red brick dust does the job perfectly. The most powerful dust is from old houses or sacred buildings, and homemade dust can be found almost everywhere. There are specialist spiritual products online, but ensure they are reputable and the dust has provenance. Lay unbroken lines across your thresholds to form psychic barriers that are impossible to cross. The most effective time to perform this ritual is the eve of the full moon, and the dust should be replaced monthly.

- **Salt:** Salt is readily available and can be removed only by evaporation. Sea salt is particularly effective, and many Hoodoo practitioners swear by the salt from the Dead Sea. Salt or saltwater can be used to solve problems with nightmares and bad dreams. Sprinkle the area around the bed with salt to remove nighttime influences and aid healthy sleep. A box filled with sea salt at your front door will protect your home and stop negative energy from entering.

- **Black salt:** This is a mixture of regular or sea salt with iron filings or charcoal. This type of salt should be used when obstructions or negative energies are particularly strong.

Air. This element is incorporated naturally in house blessings and cleanses. Burning candles or incense permeates the air while doors and windows can be opened to allow negativity to escape.

Fire. Both black and white candles bring power to your cleansing. Their potency is increased when combined with essential oils like Myrrh or Sandalwood. Use burners to protect and clean doorways and windows.

Water. Most deep cleanses are based around the element water, and it is used to wash away a multitude of ills. You can ask your local church for blessed water, or it can be purchased online.

Alternatively, You Can Bless Your Own Water with the Following Method

Step 1: Collect seawater for your cleanse. If you take it from natural sources, be sure to leave a gift for the spirits that live there. A small offering of fresh fruit or vegetables will show you are thankful for their blessings.

Step 2: Gather rainwater. Use open containers to collect fresh rainwater from your garden or windowsill. Water gathered during a thunderstorm is particularly effective. The morning dew is also used for rituals to bring revitalization to your home.

Step 3: Make your water holy. There are Hoodoo practitioners that believe in the power of moonlight, and leaving your water outside overnight renders it holy. Mix the seawater and rainwater and place the mix in a silver or glass container. Place the container on a table in the garden where it will receive the most exposure to moonlight. Charge the water with your blessings and prayers before you leave it.

Step 4: Add salt ideally, you will use a form of holy salt. Use the same phrase as you did for the water but replace the phrase "giver of life" with "preserver of life" to consecrate your salt and make it more powerful.

Step 5: *Combine the two elements. Add pinches of salt to the water while stirring in a clockwise direction. Say the final prayer,* "This holy union is blessed with the power of the elements and life. The Gods and Goddesses have made this union powerful and ready to be used in goodness and health."

Purification Baths

Purification baths are meant to purify you for the ritual you want to perform and open you up spiritually to create a channel that allows you access to the spirit world, where you can make your petition known. By doing so, purification baths increase the chances of your desires becoming a reality. But beyond opening you up, a purification bath serves other purposes, and I want to talk about a few of these right now.

<u>Severing Ties</u>

Some of us unwittingly get ourselves into sticky situations, either through love ties, ancestral curses, or as a result of our own actions. One of the many ways to get rid of such a tie is to undergo a purification bath. It helps to separate you from that person, curse, or consequence. When it comes to soul ties, you may come across an individual who is unnaturally addicted to you. Their obsession with you might have negative repercussions in your life. Even if they are not doing anything spiritual, the fact that you may have had some kind of physical interaction with them, whether through intercourse or some other shared intimate activity, may have created a tie with that person without you realizing it.

These bonds can become dangerous, especially when the person becomes obsessed with you. As for the ancestral curse, there are times when the sins of the father are visited on the son, so just because you were born to this particular individual could mean that you carry some pain and hurt in your present life as a result of that lineage. There are special baths that you can prepare to break such a tie and make sure that it ends permanently. Finally, when you offend someone, and that person holds a grudge against you, if they are the spiritual type, they could engage in declarations, sometimes through incantations and spells that will negatively affect you. Putting yourself through a purification bath will separate you from those declarations and free you from the consequences.

For Protection

As you ascend in your journey as a Hoodoo practitioner, one of the things you will realize is that a lot of the things we deal with daily are more spiritual than they are physical. The energy that people project towards you can affect you without you even realizing it. The spaces that you inhabit are not entirely new, as they belonged to previous owners. These people may have left a very negative aura in that space, and if you do not perform a purification bath, you will find yourself absorbing some of that negativity in different areas of your life. A purification bath helps to give you additional protection against these unpredictable elements. We can never predict the intentions of another, but a purification bath will protect you from them. Think of it as boosting your immune system. You might not yet be sick, but by feeding your body with the right vitamins and nutrients, you arm yourself against any disease that may want to invade your body. There may not currently be any spiritual attack or negativity in your physical space in the same way. Still, to maintain that serenity and ensure that you are well-guarded against any future attacks, a purification bath will create a barrier that keeps such things out.

CHAPTER 4: MATERIALS USED IN HOODOO

When you are ready to practice hoodoo, you must first begin gathering the tools and supplies that you are likely to require during your practices. Not all spells will require all of these supplies, but this chapter will go over the bulk of those that you will need. Remember, everything in this world has some sort of divine signature—they all have purposes, and when you learn to recognize the purposes, you will start drawing from their powers.

Baths

Maintaining purity during your attempts to communicate with the spirits is also essential to practice. Baths are viewed commonly as purifying—they are meant to help prepare you for the ritual you intend to perform, allowing you to open your mind and spirit up. Your openness then allows you to create a means of accessing the spirit world, which is how you are able to create your petition for what you want in the first place. Really, purification baths serve a very important amplification effect that you can use for your rootwork.

However, they can also be used to break ties as well. If you have made ties that are unhealthy, unnatural, or simply just negative, you can sever those ties with the bathing process. Bonds that are negative can be dangerous. Likewise, there could be occurrences in which ancestral curses fall upon you. If this happens, you can take special baths that will help to end those curses.

Candles

Candles are also incredibly prevalent in many forms of magic and religion, and they work well to help to focus energy where it is needed. When you have a candlelit, you can use it to help you to focus your psychic power where you need it. As you do so, you can then begin projecting your thoughts toward the intentions. This requires you to work on meditation while also creating and manifesting the desired intention.

Candle magic helps you to gain the clarity you need. When you have the candle present, your mind can focus, which allows you to focus effectively on the incantations or rituals you have chosen to follow to complete your spell. Of course, this is where you start seeing the power of intention working for you as well. Spells can fail or go haywire if you do not have the right intentions, and because of that, you will need to focus entirely on what you are casting. This is exactly where that candle comes in.

Herbs and Roots

Plant matter of all kinds plays an important role in hoodoo. These were some of the most traditional methods of performing magic that existed and allowed for the manifestation of those powers that were intended. They were designed to heal, protect, and defend.

The purpose of your own herbs and roots is quite important. They work in all sorts of different manners to create various effects that can very clearly change the outcomes of events in the world around you. Plants and herbs, in general, are some of the most prevalent tools that you will see in Hoodoo, and we will be dedicating a significant amount of space later to determine the various purposes of the herbs, plants, and roots that you will be able to utilize if you want to create the intended effects. Nevertheless, plants, in general, become an essential part of Hoodoo magic, and you will need to know how to wield them.

Divination Tools

Now, divination is a topic that could fill several books on its own with ease. Divination tools are various tools that will enable you to start seeing into the future to piece together the likelihood of whatever you would like to see happen. There are several different tools that are utilized for divination that all work in various ways to start spelling out the future for you before you have to do anything at all. We won't be getting into how to divine the future too much in this book just due to the sheer depth that you would need to go into. However, we will be discussing the various options that you have.

Most commonly, you see people turn to cards, bones, and candles to divine the future. When reading the cards, you are engaging in what is known as cartomancy. This is the process of reading the future through the utilization of a deck of cards. In particular, the kings and queens of the deck hold the most significance, signifying family, authorities, loved ones, and more. Through drawing the cards, you can start to understand who is being referred to in order to start piecing together what the most likely results that you will see are.

Bone reading is commonly referred to as osteomancy and is another common form of foretelling what is to come that is featured around the world. You will need a set of bones to read the future, and the ones the most commonly used were chicken or possum bones. These traditions are rooted in West Africa and remain prevalent in hoodoo. However, the tools for this task are a bit harder to get than simply using a deck of cards. If you are using the bones of an animal that you have found outside, you will need to clean and cure the bones, which is not always a very pleasant method. From there, you must bless them, and then you can start casting your bones. They are commonly cast by tossing them onto a table or other surface after asking a question. Horizontal bones are a yes, while vertical bones are a no.

Mojo Bags

Mojo bags refer to talismans or amulets. They are commonly described as a "prayer in a bag," referring to the fact that you will be casting your very own intentions when you utilize these bags. They are primarily for protection. However, there is more to it in hoodoo. In hoodoo, you will also see that there is a degree of potency included that goes a step further. The mojo bag is more along the lines of a long-term spell that you can use to focus your power. It is meant to drive that power over a period of time, allowing you to create the intended result. It is meant to be tied to who you are and the fate that you will face.

Name Papers

One thing that you will see used regularly in hoodoo is the creation of a name paper. In fact, you will see several spells that utilize them at the end of this book. Creating name papers, obviously, becomes a very important part of any hoodoo practice, so you will need to know how to make them.

Once you have the paper that you are using, you will want to write on the paper. You will write the other person's name, typically in an odd number. You want to write it in threes for manifestation, fives for domination, sevens for luck, and nines for enemy work.

Amulets and Charms

These items are used to produce vibrations and energies for the holder and the recipient of magic. They often have daily functions, yet they become magical in the right hands. Candles and holders play a significant role in certain hoodoo rituals, and it is important to have a stock of them in various colors.

Many of the most effective amulets are formed by the user and contain personal effects like hair and nail clippings to give them extra power. There are several powerful talismans connected to luck, and that are carried by gamblers and poker players. Most of these contain symbols originating from the Key of Solomon and attract power, success, and wealth.

Coyote Claws

Coyotes are known for their trickster ways, and stories tell of them stealing fire from the gods to give it to mankind, setting his tail on fire during the raid, which accounts for the markings on their tail.

Although the coyote is a rogue, he has mankind's best interest at heart. He can travel in the dark and find water in desolate places. His claw is carried by scouts and travelers who want to benefit from his skills and remain undiscovered when traveling. Claws can be purchased from select online hoodoo suppliers.

Porcupine Needles

These American needles are fun to use and can be incorporated in candles, dolls, and rootwork. They provide protection and should be placed around the object that needs protecting with the black pointy bit facing outward.

Incense

Burning incense when performing spells and rituals enhances the experience and signals the intention of the practitioner. Use a clay-burning bowl to burn your incense and self-igniting charcoal to fuel the flame.

Blends of Incense and What They Promote:

- **African juju:** Used to draw passion and intense desire into a relationship.

- **Banishing:** Remove unwanted and harmful people from your life by burning this incense when casting your spells.

- **Chuparosa:** Also known as hummingbird incense, burn it to draw your lover closer like a hummingbird seeking nectar.

- **Dragon's blood:** Containing the real blood of dragons, this resin should be burned to bring power and strength when performing rituals.

- **Has no Hanna:** This incense should be used to enhance your tools. Pass them through the smoke to enhance, charge and reenergize them before use.

- **Jinx killer:** This special blend of incense is burned to give protection from all hexes and curses sent your way.

- **Obeah:** This incense is burned by sorcerers and rootworkers who wish to communicate with the spirits.

- **Seven African Powers:** This orisha essence is used to obtain energy from Africa's seven saints.

- **Tranquility:** Burned to bring peace and harmony to your home.

Boss Fix Oil

When the hoodoo community wanted to "give it to the man" or give their boss a taste of their wrath, they would concoct a fixing oil or powder to cause discomfort when they touched certain objects like keys or doorknobs. Mixtures containing licorice, high john herbs, and other powerful herbs were used to pay back bosses who were less than kind to their staff.

This type of oil or powder can be used in modern workplaces and can be sprinkled onto their office doorknob or computer keyboard. Recite an accompanying prayer to stop them from micromanaging you and realize what a key worker you are.

Poppets

These traditional dolls are often mistaken for voodoo dolls that represent other people and that are used to cause pain. In hoodoo practices, poppets are formed from cloth or wax and represent a spirit connected to the owner. There is no malice intended when a poppet is formed, and if you treat your doll well, it will do the same for you.

When making your poppet, the color of the fabric you use will determine the powers it holds. They can be made from simple white felt and then added to, or you can choose a hue from the list below to imbue your poppet with magic:

- **Banishing:** Black fabric decorated with swords or fire.

- **Ingenuity:** Use orange or yellow fabrics with bright symbols like the sun or fire.

- **Healing:** Use spiritual colors like pale blue or white and decorate with clouds and stars.

- **Love and passion:** Red or deep pink fabric decorated with hearts and bows.

- **Wealth:** Silver or gold fabric with green trims. Decorate with dollar bills or coins and cups.

- **Protection:** Red or white material decorated with shields or keys. Use mistletoe to add an extra layer of protection.

Lodestones

Naturally occurring magnetized pieces of iron ore lodestones are used to draw positive influences toward the user. They attract love and money and are also used to direct spells away from the practitioner who has been cast by others.

Lucky Blue Balls

Known as anil in Latin American countries, these bright blue spheres are made from copper sulfate and carried for good luck. When dissolved in water, they provide a cleansing solution that will protect your house and make it a lucky place to live.

Pyrite

Known as fool's gold, this shiny mineral is widely used in Hoodoo to draw money and success to the person who carries it. Small chunks of the material can be bought for as little as $10 and make a perfect accompaniment for important attraction spells.

Coins

Certain coins play roles in Hoodoo and are often silver dollars or souvenir good luck coins. These will often have a personal attachment to the person who carries them. In the 1930s, at the height of the Great Depression, these coins were manufactured to bring luck to people who were suffering. They feature horseshoes, four-leaf clover, and other symbols of good luck. Most of the coins have no monetary value and can be found online or in traditional shops selling hoodoo paraphernalia.

Mojo Beans

Also known as wishing beans and African mojo beans, these are classic good luck talismans and should be carried in a piece of red material to bring the holder good fortune.

Twice Stricken Lightning Wood

This is a popular tool in Hoodoo and is a powder ground from wood that has been struck by lightning. It has powers of attraction that can be used for sexual spells and commanding a lover to return. It also has cleansing properties as the lightning represents the power of purity and transformation.

Bones

Throwing the bones is one of the most traditional forms of divination and is part of hoodoo-style worship. The bones used will all have a meaning, and how the throw is interpreted will depend on the person who casts them. The bone reader should cast a petition to the gods describing what they need to know before casting the bones to the mat or animal skin covering a table.

Many people believe that the further away the bones fall means they depict things from the future while the closest bones relate to the present. Spaces between the bones or the shapes they make all have relevance.

If you intend to perform this divination rite, it is important to have a variety of natural bones and other objects to cast. Include items like:

- The arm from a china doll

- Alligator foot

- Sharks' tooth

- Dog ankle bone

- Shell from nutmeg

- Snake vertebra

- Raccoon penis bone

- Rabbit rib bone

- Abalone shell

- Cowrie shell

- Vintage keys

- Ravens' claw

- Chickens' foot

This is just a selection of items you can use to throw the bones. Add jewelry or personal items to make the reading more relevant to whoever wants their questions answered.

Abramelin Oil

Abramelin Oil is a magical ceremonial oil mixed with aromatic plants. It is so-called because its description is in a medieval grimoire called "The Book of Abramelin", written by Abraham of Worms. The recipe is adapted from the Holy Jewish Oil of Tanakh, which is described in the book of Exodus attributed to Moses.

Much has been written about this oil. In the Jewish tradition, from which the original biblical recipe for oil derives, the olive is a symbol of happiness and domestic stability, myrrh is considered sacred to the Lord, the aromatic calamus is known for its sweetness, and the phallic shape of its fruit represents male sexuality and love, while cinnamon is favored for its warming power. Crowley also had a symbolic vision of the ingredients he found in Mathers' translation:

Spirits

Spirits are the foundation of hoodoo, one of the few "strong" beliefs that is present and is also one of the sine qua non-conditions without which hoodoo becomes an act without reasoned basis. Spirits are those of the dead, linked to acts, people and places but rarely with a specific connotation. The simplest thing to define the spirits of hoodoo is to consider the rules that govern them. In fact, they are subject, in tradition, to precise limitations, just as the living are.

They influence and regulate everyday life, they are part of the human community, they move and act with precise purposes and according to desires similar to those of the living. So a spirit will not be able to cross a bridge, a living watercourse (like a river), a busy road or some "magic" barriers (lines of brick or white salt dust, for example, or points where specific prayers have been said) unless the root doctor removes these barriers making them ineffective through his magic. Spirits cannot enter a house unless they are called from within. They will be drawn by specific invocations, prayers and artifacts, driven out and exorcised by equally specific invocations, artifacts and prayers. They will love offerings of money, candles and food, chili and pepper, but they will hate salt and will want to be paid for every job done so much so that they will take a payment due if it is not paid.

The sacred space

In the practice of the root doctor, the sacred space is a natural rather than consecrated place, which takes shape in the place and time of the magic operation and ceases to be particular at the end of the operation. Sacred places are the crossroads and the cemetery, but any room or place becomes one. For quick operations, such as lighting a candle rubbed with various oils or building a bag full of amulets, complex consecrations, ceremonial precautions, symbolic protections are not used. The two-headed doctor is immersed in the spiritual world he is part of, and in practice, the hoodoo operation is immediate and simple. The spirits know him, and he pays them for their services with offerings and prayers, and that is that. However, even in complex operations, it is rare that "ceremonial circles" or "invocation triangles" are built in the European way to protect themselves from apparitions of spirits because, in these places, the spirits are always free and present. Just think that a handful of cemetery land is considered to contain a spirit and that some root doctors have dozens of jars (depending on the graves they have visited, to use them in different spells).

Vinegar of the Four Thieves

Four Thieves vinegar is widely used in Hoodoo. It can be used for personal protection, disease prevention, banishing unwanted people from your life, and casting curses.

Legend has it that the recipe dates back to the origin of a band of thieves in the Middle Ages. The thieves were in the habit of robbing victims of the Black Plague. Upon arrest, they revealed the secret of not catching the plague: four vinegar thieves. This is an interesting story, but it is more likely that "the vinegar of the four thieves" is a corruption of "Fort have's Vinegar," which had been used as a remedy for centuries.

Also known as Marseille vinegar, the potion varies widely among manufacturers. There are two general classes, one for internal use and another strictly for external use. The solution can contain any number of herbs. However, almost all recipes say there must be a minimum of four additives, one for each of the thieves.

Vinegar is used as both an attractant and repellent because it has the ability to absorb negative energy. Sulfur powder is thought to have magical properties such as the power to draw money, love or luck. Additionally, it can be used for protection from evil influences and witchcraft. Cat hair is one of the most common ingredients used in hoodoo spells because the cat represents strong will and power. It is believed to be lucky to have a cat in the house.

Components:

- 1 gallon of apple cider vinegar

- 1 fl. oz. thyme

- 1 fl. oz. word phrase

- 1 fl. oz. lavender

- 1 fl. oz. camphor powder

- 1 fl. oz. wise sage

- 1 fl. oz. mint peppermint

- 1 fl. oz. lilac grass

<u>**Vinegar of the Four Thieves spell**</u>

This is a spell designed to banish, that is to say, drive someone away or make them disappear from our lives. It includes punishment for the victim if they do not satisfy your desire to leave your life. Obviously, there has to be a right motive, not a purer spell.

Needed:

- A black candle

- Crossing or hexing oil

- A small bottle of vinegar

- A lemon

- A glass jar

- Pins

- Photo of the person

How to Proceed:

First step, purify everything with fumigations of sage or rosemary.

Then proceed by engraving the person's name on the candle and then greasing it. As you anoint the candle, say "(name) that all the evil you have done to me now may come back to you!" Being a spell to banish the candle, pay attention.

Put the candle in a holder and light it with a fire returned. Write the person's name three times in small letters on the picture, then cross it and cover it with the words "AGRO E AMARO" in large letters and bold. Fold the photo three times, turning it counterclockwise between each fold, saying, "The presence and influence of X (name) in my life that is forever away from me!

Cut a slice in the lemon, insert the photo and close it. Stick the lemon with the pins and pronounce "(name)" while inserting each pin "shut your mouth or shut up or leave".

Put the lemon in the jar and fill the jar with vinegar. Screw the lid on tightly, shake the jar and say "(name)":

"Sir, while you were showing the blind, show (name) that you didn't put it in my life! How did the lame man walk, let (name) walk away from my life forever! As you cast the demons out of the possessed, cast them out of my life forever! Lord, may your life become as bitter as this lemon and as bitter as this vinegar with each passing day until you leave my life forever! As this lemon rots, so will its health and vitality rot until it leaves my life forever! In the name of Jesus. Amen."

Leave the jar next to the candle until it is consumed, then when you have finished, bury the jar in a cemetery or throw it in a body of water. As long as the person stays out of your life and business, nothing will happen to them. But they continue to creep into your life, the curse will take hold. The choice is up to them.

Black powder

Black powder is an evocation potion composed of cemetery dirt and various additives, such as snakeskin or salt. The name comes from the Bantu word kufua, which means "to die." It is used as a curse or to hurt someone. A black bag is worn to protect against such attacks.

Black powder is spread in the path of the intended victim or applied to a pillow, person or the edges of one's home. The first sign of being targeted is sharp pains in the feet and legs, followed by swelling and inability to walk. These symptoms are almost identical to complications of diabetes.

Black Powder Spell

Purpose: for protecting stationary or inanimate objects like your home, jewelry or even the area where you cast your spell. You can also use it as a protection spell for a person

Protection spells commonly use circles. In Hoodoo magic, drawing circles is a form of basic ritualistic practice. You use certain elements to create circles around what you are blessing, cursing, protecting or empowering with your spell. It is no different in this situation. The black salt that you create should be used in a circle around the person object or space that you want to protect. Here is what you need:

- Black pepper

- Charcoal

- Salt

- Wood ash

Put all ingredients together in a mortar and grind them using the same movement as the clock hand. Ensure that everything mixes smoothly and evenly. Empty the contents into a bowl and bless it with a prayer from Psalm 91. Use the salt powder to make circles around anything or any person you want to protect.

Dislodging the Spirit from the Client

Before you start to meddle with the customer, start by protecting yourself. You ought to have the two feet, two hands, your forehead, heart, navel, and the rear of your neck blessed with Fiery Protection Oil. Furthermore, I recommend you call the entirety of your protective entities and spirits to take care of you. At long last, ensure you are donning white or comparatively light-colored clothes to ensure you are very much protected. On the off chance that you have a Protection Mojo Bag, convey it.

Since everything is set up, you're ready to start. Start by lighting the stogie and ensuring you have decent consuming ash toward the end. Flip the stogie around and put the lit end into your mouth, and blow through the stogie to drive smoke out of it toward your customer. Utilize the smoke to cajole the spirit that is assaulting them to approach. Then, at that point, get the heap of herbs, blow some stogie smoke onto it, and ask either Psalm 51 (beneath) or The Lord's Prayer:

Show benevolence upon me, O God, as indicated by thy lovingkindness: agreeing unto a large number of thy delicate kindnesses abrogate my transgressions.

Wash me thoroughly from mine evildoing, and cleanse me from my transgression.

For I recognize my transgressions: and my wrongdoing is ever before me.

Against you, you just, have I trespassed and done this evil in thy sight: that thou mightest be defended when thou speakest and be clear when thou judgest.

Observe, I was sharpened in injustice; and in wrongdoing did my mom consider me.

See, thou desires truth in the internal parts: and in the secret part thou shalt make me know insight.

Cleanse me with hyssop, and I will be clean: wash me, and I will be more white than snow.

Make me hear bliss and happiness; that the bones which thou hast broken may rejoice.

Cover up thy face from my transgressions, and scratch out the entirety of mine injustices.

Create in me a clean heart, O God; and renew a right spirit inside me.

Cast me not away from thy presence, and take not thy Essence of God from me.

Restore unto me the delight of thy salvation, and maintain me with thy free spirit.

Then, at that point will I instruct transgressors thy ways; and delinquents will be changed over unto you.

Convey me from bloodguiltiness, O God, thou God of my salvation: and my tongue will sing so anyone might hear of thy honorableness.

O Lord, open thou my lips; and my mouth will shew forward thy acclaim.

For thou desirest not penance; else would I give it: thou delightest not in the consumed offering.

The penances of God are a messed up spirit: a wrecked and a humble heart, O God, thou shrivel not loathe.

Do good in thy good pleasure unto Zion: fabricate thou the dividers of Jerusalem.

Then, at that point shalt thou be satisfied with the penances of honesty, with consumed offering and entire consumed offering: then, at that point will they offer bullocks upon thine special stepped area.

Presently, gradually turn the customer and softly whack their body with the help of herbs. As you do as such, order the spirit to leave that person's body and to let them be for the sake of Jesus Christ, Amen. Start at their head, and work your direction down toward the feet. (Ensure you don't disturb the twisting of memorial park soil and black powder.) Once you have reached the feet, move over to the jug and blow some stogie smoke into the container and around it to cajole the spirit to advance toward the jug. Presently addressing the spirit directly, express that you have created another home for it, one where it can appreciate a good beverage and a good smoke - over in their bottle.

Catching the Spirit

Presently, supplicating the Lord's Prayer, again and again, take the stogie and light the black powder nearest to the customer with the goal that the copy will be winding out and away from him toward the jug, pushing the spirit to leave the body and go into the jug. Shoo it alongside the heap of herbs as the starting fire moves along. At the point when the black powder completes the process of consuming around the jug, rapidly cap the container and state out loud: "Spirit, I have caught you in the tangled wreck in this jug. Nevermore can you get away from this container, and never again will you inconvenience another spirit! In Jesus' name AMEN!" Wrap the jug in dark cloth and tie the opposite corners firmly over the highest point of the jug with the goal that it won't ever come around again.

Cascarilla (Croton Eluteria)

If you have got a legal battle coming up and do not know if you will win it, you will probably turn to cascara sagrada bark. By creating an infusion and surrounding your property before your court case, you will help to protect yourself. Or, you can also burn it on charcoal the day before your case to up your chances of victory.

Peace Rituals: Using Dirt and Minerals

I mentioned using *dirt from a church* in a mojo bag for love, but this can also be used to bring peace to your home or place of work (if these two spaces aren't one and the same).

Chalk or *Cascarilla* (pronounced kaws-kuh-ree-uh). An inexpensive powder made of eggshells that can be added to workings or sprinkled around a space.

Peace Powder. Sometimes this is the same as Cascarilla, but you can also find botanicals that make unique blends. For use in the home or at work.

Coffin Nails

These are used in conjure work to drive away or harm an enemy.

Colognes and Perfumes

There are various colognes made by non-Hoodoo firms that are employed by practitioners because of their magical and spiritual properties.

Florida Water, Strong Love, Kananga Water, Hoyt's Cologne, and Jockey Club are some of the most popular colognes. Colognes may be used to cleanse items and people while also providing protection and good luck. The Jockey Club became well-known for its ability to bring about good fortune and employment. Hoyt's Cologne is one of the most well-known Hoodoo colognes. Hoyt's is said to offer gamblers good luck. Both Kananga Water and Florida Water are well-known for their usage in Hoodoo protection and purification rituals. Hoodoo perfumes are used to "attract" certain energies based on their aroma and color. Perfumes can be used to attract luck or money and to hex or remove curses.

Coon Bone

The bone extracted from a raccoon's penis is treasured as a lucky charm. The bone is thought to be beneficial in concerns of love and gambling. These bones were discovered in slave quarters in both Tennessee and Virginia.

Dimes

The silver from a dime can alleviate pain when drilled and threaded through a piece of red thread. Wearing a dime around one's neck or ankle will protect the wearer from being "tricked."

Floor Washes

Floor washes are liquids containing various fluids, oils, and plants that are used to "mop" spaces where spiritual activity can be done.

Goofer Dust

Goofer dust is used to perform tricks on adversaries. It might be strewn in an area where the sufferer would be exposed to the dust. The victim is drawn to the victim by the dust, which draws the souls of the deceased. Graveyard dirt, sulfur, brimstone, and salt are all traditional ingredients. Snake and lizard skins, as well as red peppers, are among the variations. The name "goofer" is an abbreviation for the African word kuwfa, which means "dead person." Slave superstition said that if a slave wore burial soil in his shoes, he would not be spotted by dogs.

Gunpowder

Gunpowder can be used to call spirits or put a spell in motion.

Horseshoes

Horseshoes are classic good luck symbols. They are thought to be able to fend off ghosts, witches, and conjurers in Hoodoo culture. They were widely used to cover the entrances to homes and businesses.

Lodestones

These are amulets used for protection and attracting success. To attract funds, they might be "dressed" with "Money Drawing" oil. Magnetic sand is "fed" to lodestones to put them to work. Lodestones are said to exist in both male and female versions. Giving iron filings to the male is known as "feeding the he," while feeding the female is known as "feeding the she." "Lucky Bingo" is used to increase gaming success. Citronella is present in "Fast Luck" oil, which may be utilized to attract consumers to a business. In operations, "Come to Me," and "Drawing" oils are used to attract the opposite sex. According to Zora Neale Hurston, Van Van oil was once the most popular conjuring medicine in Louisiana. The oil is thought to bestow luck and power on those who use it. It is also said to be capable of removing tricks. Oils such as "Prosperity," "Triple Fast Luck," "Fast Success," and "Lucky 13" are said to bring financial benefits. Oils used to counteract bad effects such as hexes include "Cast Off Evil," "Stop Evil," and "Jinx Remover." "Double Cross" can be used to "turn back" trickery.

Powders

Powders are referred to be "spiritual sachet powers." These are usually made of talc mixed with various herbs and colors. Powders can be dusted and blown into specified areas to clear negativity or bring about positive outcomes. There are several powders used in Hoodoo culture, including "Attraction Powder," which is used to attract love into your life; "Magnet Powder," which is used to attract good health and luck; "Money Drawing Powder," which is used to bring financial success; and "Uncrossing Powder," which is used to remove curses, among others. "Hot Foot Powder," which is meant to drive adversaries and undesired persons away, is one powder that has garnered prominence in the Hoodoo tradition. "You will take the Hot Foot Powder and sprinkle of this powder at a place where your enemy will walk so that the fever to move will take hold of them and enter their body and they will become dissatisfied with their place of living and move away and not bother either you or your good neighbors anymore," anthropologist Zora Neale Hurston told her readers. Sonny Boy Brand Jinx Remover is a popular powder among practitioners, with the label stating, "The purported abilities of Sonny Boy are limited only by your own faith." The advantages of good fortune and prosperity are available via spiritual strength and power."

Quicksilver

Mercury is utilized to ward off the evil eye. Also, it is used to speed up the work of spirits in several African-based faiths. To get good luck in gaming, conjurers would drill a hole in a piece of nutmeg and fill it with quicksilver.

Rabbit's Foot

The rabbit's foot is said to bring good luck and was previously used to ward off evil spirits. To relieve a fever, some rootworkers advised customers to put their foot on a string around their neck.

Red Brick Dust

Crushed bricks are ground into a powder, and the resulting powder is utilized to create magical protection. There are several testimonials in Hoodoo tradition regarding devotees who put red brick dust at the entryway of a home to protect it.

Salt

Salt is mostly used for protection.

Scissors

Scissors are used to "cutaway" crossings and protection.

CHAPTER 5: ROOTWORK AND HOW TO USE HERBS AND ROOTS IN YOUR MAGIC

Rootwork

In its earliest days, hoodoo was called many different things. One of the terms for healing that the first conjurers practiced was called 'rootwork,' 'mojo,' 'conjure,' 'folk magick,' or 'mojo.'

There are also different names for magickal practices similar to hoodoo. For example, what's known as hoodoo in the United States would be called 'obeah' in Jamaica.

We used to use plants for healing. Many indigenous cultures still do. One of the more common ways plants are still used in this way is with teas. You probably have a selection of teas in your kitchen cabinet right now that can be used for one purpose or another.

To practice seriously, you'll need to do more than spend a few minutes researching. Smell the plants, herbs, and roots you have. Feel them. Look at them to know how they appear so you can tell one dried or fresh plant from the next.

You may already know the taste from cooking and drinking, but ideally, you get to a point where you can tell a plant (and know its properties useful for your work) by looking at it.

Often beginning practitioners have a list of things they go out and buy for their first spell. While this is fine when it comes to working, hoodoo is about being connected to plants, roots, and herbs. It is the root in rootwork.

This might mean a lot of research and time for you at first, but really what you're doing is connecting yourself to the spirit of the earth. You don't want to rush this just for the sake of getting to whatever spell you want to work. The relationship you develop is a lifelong one and will serve you for years to come.

After your teas, do some research on the spices you have, the plants and flowers growing in your backyard or in pots. Next, you may want to look into how you can grow more herbs on your own. Eventually getting to the point where you don't have to buy a plant for a working.

The Power of Dirt

Just like you wouldn't throw any plant inside of working without knowing what the plant is and why you're using it, you wouldn't collect and use dirt from just anywhere.

Especially not a graveyard.

As discussed in the section Working with Place, dirt from different locations can help with our magic. Aside from graveyards, these are common:

- Hospitals

- Churches

- Banks

- Colleges or Universities

- Courthouses

- Casinos

- Rivers

Folks definitely get creative when it comes to collecting dirt. Any place you come across has a spirit, and that spirit gets into the soil around and underneath. With the right process, you could technically collect dirt from anywhere, not just the ones listed above.

There is dirt and dust used in hoodoo that doesn't come from a specific place but is tied to a circumstance or situation. One example is anvil dust, which is commonly substituted with magnetic dust in many spells. These two things are not the same.

Anvil dust is specifically collected from what is leftover in a blacksmith's shop, where hard work happens and direct focus is necessary. Anvil dust is infused with that spirit.

Taking dirt from a place is taking some of the power for your own purposes, so before going out to collect dirt, you want to know why you're taking dirt and what you plan to do with it.

You also want to take with you something to leave in place of whatever you took. Coins are a common offering, as is rum or whisky. If you don't want to leave anything or disturb the roots, you can clean up any garbage left in the area and leave the space better than you found it.

Collecting graveyard dirt isn't for the novice practitioner, but if you venture out, you want to collect at the right time. Take note of the cycle of the moon and time of day. As a general guide, collecting after midnight and in the early morning hours is best.

Another consideration is the exact location of the dirt collected, again, this is especially true when collecting graveyard dirt. Depending on your spell, you may want to collect dirt underneath a shadow, at the entrance or the four corners of the graveyard.

Roots at Home

Growing some of your own plants not only gives you access to the plants but gives you the opportunity to influence the energies in the plant itself. Using blessed water on a plant can purify its power.

There are also practices that show plants respond to positive speech and energies. This gives us the opportunity to practice prayer in an unconventional way, as we can begin to pray to the plant itself.

I would also look into a greenhouse or outdoor storage of some sort, as certain plants need warmer, damper conditions to grow, and, thus, during colder months, they are harder to get hold of.

This greenhouse could also be a place where you can store bags of soil or any items you've collected that you may not want in the house, such as chicken bones.

Hanging protection stones or painting symbols on and in the greenhouse will also keep unwanted spirits from your materials.

By the way, don't panic if you have no plant pots, like jars, jugs, and old plastic tubs work just as well for planting with very alterations. In fact, you could grab a small plastic tub, put some soil in it, and grow mint on any windowsill in your home.

The key here is to make an effort. There is a big difference between "wanting" and "doing" and between "saying" and "doing." And the spirits will see this; someone who truly wants to do something but who is not actually acting may not be in favor of the spirits.

Cleaning Your Roots

Remove the soil and dirt gently and with care. An old toothbrush is perfect as it can remove the dirt without removing the tiny hairs that cover the roots. These hairs are packed with important constituents that need to be preserved.

Any cutting needs to be done when fresh as dry roots are difficult to cut cleanly. Once you have cut your roots to the required size, you need to dry them sympathetically. This can be done by laying the cuttings on trays placing them outside out of direct sunlight but in a warm atmosphere. You can use a food dehydrator on a low setting of 150 degrees or a regular oven on a low setting with the door left open.

Quick Note: Some roots will attract moisture and become soft, discard any limp or flaccid roots immediately.

There are different rituals for charging your herbs and roots and preparing them for rootwork, so here is a general tutorial you can adapt for your uses:

- Place your herbs and roots on a sacred surface and bless them with a prayer or psalm

- Use a smudging stick to bless the offerings

- Leave the roots and herbs outside in the light of the full moon

- Place the roots and herbs in a container filled with sacred salt

Herbal Magic

Although many adherents of modern hoodoo practices are African-American, there are also many non-black practitioners. However, the roots of the tradition are typically found in the folkloric practices of Central and West Africa and were carried to the United States during the slave trade period. These magical systems are sometimes known as Hoodoo but are also called conjure or rootwork, depending on the practitioner.

Many Hoodoo spells are linked to love and lust, money and gambling, and other functional applications. There is also, in some ways of Hoodoo, a veneration of ancestors. However, it is important to note that despite the use of magic and ancestor worship, Hoodoo is by no means a pagan tradition—many practitioners are, in fact, Christians, and some even use the Psalms as a starting point for sorcery.

A list of some common roots, barks and wood, leaves, and herbs that are commonly used in hoodoo.

There are a few different ways these can be used in your magic.

- ***As an offering to your ancestors or to deities.*** Many of the seeds, plants, roots, and herbs we use regularly were also used by our ancestors. Usually about half a teaspoon of herbs or seeds can be added onto a small plate and left on the altar once offered.

- ***Burned as an incense.*** It's much easier to do this with some herbs and roots than others. Burning can heighten the vibration of space and prepare an environment before a ritual or spell.

- ***Added to your working.*** One of the easiest ways to use the power of seeds, roots, barks, leaves, and herbs is by adding them to a mojo bag, hoodoo lamp, or jar or bottle.

- ***Dressing candles.*** In rituals or prior to meditation, some hoodoo spells require the dressing of a candle, though you can also dress any candle that you're getting ready to use. If you've set an intention for the day, for example, looking for a job, you can dress a candle with herbs that can help and let it burn while you're going about your day.

When you start your practice, you'll soon discover it can be hard to keep track of what you have in your hoodoo pantry. Here's where keeping a magical record is useful. Some traditions would call this a 'book of shadows.'

There isn't really a hoodoo equivalent to a book of shadows, and it doesn't take long to figure out why. Keeping a diary of magick is something people who have the privilege of privacy do. This is why, in starting your hoodoo practice, you want to recognize that you can read a book like this or keep notes and not be in trouble should someone else discover what you're doing.

All this to say, if you're reading this, I'm pretty sure you can get a binder or some other notebook to write down how you're progressing in your practice.

Section out a few pages to keep track of what herbs you have in stock and if you'll need to resupply soon. Alternatively, you can keep a digital list of some sort. These can help with marking which items you need to get and when your stock is running low.

The point is to find a system that works. You don't want to go out to buy something only to get home and find you had it already.

Seeds

- ***Caraway.*** Can be used to stop someone you love from straying away, is also helpful for increasing mental powers, bringing in love, passion, and is said to be anti-theft. Offer on a love altar or add some seeds to a mojo bag.

- ***Cardamom.*** For increasing the love in your life. Particularly useful to soothe your own heart if you've been hurt or in pain. Can help with your luck in love and fidelity.

- ***Celery.*** If placed under a pillow, can encourage prophetic dreams while sleeping also increases psychic abilities and helps with concentration.

- ***Coriander.*** Commonly used in love spells, for lust, can be added to wine in ground form (though be careful with this). Can be used to ease the pain of a breakup. Great for mojo bags or dressing candles ahead of love rituals.

- ***Cumin.*** Can be used to keep evil away, curse enemies, or increase fidelity in your relationships. Can also be used to prevent theft and for protection. Can be burned on a charcoal disc and used in workings.

- ***Fennel.*** Use these if you are going through hard times and need some extra support. Good for healing spells.

Also works in purification, strength, and protection. Tie in a satchel and hang it in your home to protect your space from evil and unwanted energies.

- *Fenugreek.* Commonly used for drawing in money. One way to use it is to keep some seeds in an open container on a kitchen counter or table and add seeds to it over time. Can also be used in the home by adding seeds to floor washes.

- *Flax.* Can help to ward off any harsh or angry energies. Used in spells for healing and drawing in money. Also called Linseed. Combine with a few coins and place on an altar for financial stability.

- *Mustard.* Different types have different uses. White or yellow seeds are usually associated with faith, as the bible verse says. Yellow mustard seeds can be carried in a small bottle or amulet for faith and success.

- *Poppy.* The highly potent drug opium is extracted from these seeds, which aligns with how it can be used in magic: to help with getting rest and feeling pleasure. Can also be used to confuse enemies or people who are in your way. Carry some seeds in a mojo bag or satchel.

- *Star Anise.* Can increase your psychic ability and awareness. Carried to increase your luck and is said to be able to keep the evil eye away. Also used in money magic.

Excellent for container spells or carried for luck, protection, and divination.

Roots

- ***Adam & Eve Root.*** Available in two; one root is shaped like a large marble with a flat side, and the other is shaped like a large nail. Together, these roots can be used to attract love to you. If you're in a relationship, each partner can carry one of the roots to keep your union strong. These roots come from orchid plants, which are endangered in many parts of the United States.

- ***Althaea.*** A protective healer. Use in your spells when you or someone else needs to ease a broken heart or any emotional discord. It is said to draw spirits to you that will help in whatever you need. Can be burned on a charcoal disc.

- ***Angelica.*** The root of angels. This is often said to help women with feeling strong and protected. Add to a bath or personal skincare products, grow in a garden or balcony to protect your home.

- ***Bat's Head.*** Also called Devil Pod, Vampire Root, and Cat's Claw. This is an actual pod that appears to have eyes and a mouth. It looks a little scary but is considered a favorite among hoodoo workers. Used primarily for protection, but also has powers in granting wishes.

- **Dandelion.** For strengthening psychic abilities. A plant that can aid in transformation and abundance. If you live in an area where there are many of these plants, forage for your own instead of buying from a supplier. Be aware, dandelion leaves have slightly different uses than the root.

- **Calamus.** To gain control over yourself or get the upper hand in situations where you need it. Also great for protection. Often used in work that has to do with domination, casting a spell, or added to oils.

- **Culver.** A major purifier. Other names for this root are Bowman's Root, Brinton Root, Culver's Physic, and Physic Root (yes, that's physic, and not psychic). If you need spiritual purification beyond what you can do on your own, an experienced practitioner may use this root.

- **Ginger.** A root that is amazing for building confidence and going out into a brave new world. Next time you're in the market for ginger root, look for one that is shaped like a human—this is said to be a powerful magical tool. Use to add fire and speed to spells.

- **Ginseng.** Used for various magical purposes, including protection, healing, love, sex, and general luck.

Famously used to boost male virility. Burn to keep evil spirits away or carry to draw luck to you.

- ***Gravel Root.*** For help in getting and maintaining a job. Additionally, it can be used to ease distress, so if you are having trouble at work, this root may be an ideal option. Best used when carried, especially while working.

- ***Jezebel.*** Said to be used by sex workers to draw clients who are submissive and give good tips. Can be used equally well for cursing an enemy. Use in a money-drawing mojo bag or honey jar.

- ***Licorice.*** Generally used in spells about love and relationships. However, it is also often used for spells with the intent of gaining control. Can be carried to attract love or chewed to build confidence.

- ***Mandrake.*** Another common all-purpose root used for wealth, health, love, and protection. As its name suggests, this root is shaped like a man and said to 'scream' when it is harvested. Keep in your home, on a mantel or altar, for protection. Place on top of money for financial abundance.

- ***Valerian.*** For peace, harmony, love, and protection. May be helpful in situations where there's discord in a relationship. Also known as 'Vandal'. Can be burned, to hex, or burned with a yellow candle to clear a hex cast on you.

- **_Verbena._** An all-purpose. Noted to help with all of the usual life situations: money, love, protection, healing, and peace. Additionally, helpful with maintaining youth, helping with low vibrations, and increasing creativity. Also known as 'Vervain.' Include in prosperity spells or carry with you when you need to be creative.

From Trees

- **_Cedar._** There's some disagreement on how this wood can help with your magic, but it's generally said to be protective and helpful with matters of the home. Available as wood chips, branches are also used in incense. Can be burned for cleansing in the same way as sage and palo santo.

- **_Frankincense._** A massively powerful resin used in nearly all types of spells to boost their power. Usually burned on a charcoal disc to clear a space and to heighten vibration, so excellent to use ahead of rituals where you need extra power. Resin can also be offered to ancestors and deities on your altar.

- **_Myrrh._** Another powerful resin that can be used in the same way as Frankincense. Associated with Isis. Used for

spiritual healing, to raise vibrations ahead of meditation
or rituals. Excellent for blessing your space and magical
tools and is a connector to the dead.

- ***Pine Needles.*** An alternative to palo santo if you're in
  need of spiritual cleansing. In addition, said to attract
  prosperity. Pine trees survive in harsh conditions and are
  worth a try if you need some of that resilience in you or
  your magic.

Leaves

- ***Acacia.*** Used in spiritual practices and rites for
  thousands of years in cultures around the world. A
  masculine all-purpose plant that can be used to clean
  and consecrate your magical tools. Burn, or use in
  washes.

- ***Agrimony.*** A spell reverser. If you think or know
  someone has hexed you, this leaf can help and dissolve
  the things that can get in your way: depression, anger,
  sadness, fear, impatience, *etc*. Use in body washes and in
  oils.

- ***Alfalfa.*** A leaf commonly used for money and financial
  abundance. In addition, it's also said to keep away
  poverty and hunger. Dispersing under a carpet in your

home may help with attracting clients and customers for your at-home business,

- ***Basil.*** All-purpose: love, cleansing, protection, attracting money, love, and abundance, must-have for any serious practitioner. Widely available in North America considered sacred in some cultures. To use for blessing your home with prosperity and happiness, soak some dried herbs in water for three days. Strain and sprinkle the water by your door.

- ***Bay.*** Another all-purpose leaf that many practitioners across many different magical practices use regularly. Particularly effective at keeping evil away, specifically when dealing in hexes and curses. Write what you want on a leaf and burn it to draw in your desires. Excellent to purify the air (by burning) if someone sick has been in a room.

- ***Catnip.*** Used for love, particularly by women who want to attract a specific man. Can also be useful in mojo bags for physical attractiveness and self-love. Can be carried to attract someone to you. Hang dried over your door to draw in luck and good spiritual energy.

- ***Damiana.*** Another leaf used for love and lust specifically. Also used to increase psychic ability and to help align the chakras. Helps build the energy of other magical herbs. Use as an offering on a love altar or in sachets, honey jars, mojo bags, or candle working to draw love to you.

- **_Holly._** Used for protection and drawing luck. The same leaf is often associated with Christmas, so you'll find it hanging in practitioners' homes during Yule. Can draw protection for the home when burned with incense. Often used around Christmas time.

- **_Lemon._** Lemon leaves have similar magical properties to the fruit. Very effective for cleansing negative energy, especially from old or reused items. Leaves can be used for cleansing, either your body or home.

- **_Oregano._** An herb commonly used in food can also be protective and give your magick some added energy. Oregano leaves have been burned for centuries to keep negative energies away.

- **_Passion Flower._** Doesn't quite arouse passion but is useful in love spells and for building your social circle. Promotes sleep when placed under a pillow.

- **_Patchouli._** A masculine leaf that's useful for money and for love. Is also reported to be useful for breaking spells cast on you by someone else. Often used in spells, oils, and bags for love and for money. Can be placed in your wallet to draw money.

- **_Rosemary._** Another leaf used by many practitioners, particularly by women. Can both heal and protect. Also said to be useful in the home, particularly when hung dried over a window or door. Use to draw love or healing by creating a poppet of yourself and filling it with this herb.

- **_Sage._** Like Palo Santo, Sage is a leaf used for cleansing, blessing, and purification. Certain types of sage are specifically sacred to Native American cultures.

- **_Violet._** Can be worn to keep a calm temperament and stay peaceful. May also help with drawing in love. Place leaves in a green mojo bag or sachet to heal physical and emotional wounds, and protect yourself when wounded.

Herbs

- **_Asafetida._** Said to help with repelling evil and can be used to bring difficulties to your enemies. Does not smell nice. Burn on charcoal and say your petition in the name of the devil to stop someone from bothering you.

- **_Calendula._** A flower used for psychic and spiritual powers, boosting your luck, and getting help when it comes to legal matters. Can be placed in a garland on your door to keep evil away. Useful in love working or as an offering on a love altar.

- ***Chamomile.*** Widely used for healing, to diminish stress and clean an environment of any hexes, curses or lingering energy. Also useful for luck, bringing in money, and attracting love. Use in a bath for love.

- ***Cinnamon.*** A fiery spice that can be burned for heightened spiritual abilities, for prosperity, and to raise your vibration. Beneficial for drawing in money and success. If you have cinnamon, burn it! It can draw money and love, purify, and aid your psychic abilities.

- ***Cinquefoil.*** Can be useful when you're dealing with legal bodies, since it helps with finding your words. Five points represent love, money, power, health, and wisdom, and it's said this herb will impart those on anyone who wears it.

- ***Cloves.*** Can be used for any magick related to fire (i.e. your willpower). Helps with money, love, and protection. Burning cloves as incense can work to attract money and raise vibrations.

- ***Elder.*** Roots, leaves, berries, and flowers are major for protection but are also poisonous, so be careful. Can be used to guard your home and your money-making endeavors. Can be worn for protection.

- ***Garlic.*** Widely used to protect against all forms of evil, including vampires (energetic or otherwise). Healing and great for exorcising negative energies or entities. Hanging in the home won't protect against vampires but will boost your willpower and strengthen family bonds.

- ***Hops.*** This beer flower is excellent in magick to help induce sleep and pleasant dreams. Also beneficial in healing and money magic. Use in dream pillows or to help with inducing restful sleep.

- ***Hyssop.*** A mint mentioned in the bible (Psalm 51) for spiritual purification. Highly popular in magick for cleansing, particularly for washes and baths. Soak in water for a few days, strain and use the water to cleanse your magical tools and objects.

- ***Jasmine.*** A flower that is good for attracting a soul mate and generally being open to love. Also useful for divination, drawing wealth, and charging crystals (quartz specifically).

- ***Juniper Berry.*** Used for attracting love and increasing attraction and lust. It keeps things you don't want away and has the ability to attract good vibrations and health.

- ***Lavender.*** A flower used to attract love, heal from depression. Promotes sleep and can help with purification. Highly popular as an essential oil. Burning the flowers and spreading ashes can help with love spells and rituals.

- ***Mugwort.*** Often used to cleanse and purify tools used for divination, such as scrying mirrors. Can also help with fertility. Create a Mugwort 'tea' (or infusion) by mixing one teaspoon of the herb with one cup of boiling water and using this to clean your altar and magical tools.

- ***Nettle.*** Nature's 'Return to Sender'. Return any spells or hexes cast on you, build your will, strengthen yourself and your ability to handle emergencies.

- ***Nutmeg.*** Whole helps with luck and winning at games where luck is needed. Can also be used to attract prosperity, protection, and help to break a hex. Sprinkle on a green or white candle for use in prosperity spells, use in mojo bags, and satchels.

- ***Red Pepper.*** Crushed or pods, have the same correspondence, cleansing and triggering a breakup of a relationship. Used for 'enemy' magic, to drive someone away or cause bad luck to someone else, often with other herbs like salt and black pepper.

- ***Rose.*** The love flower. As a rose has its thorns, so does this flower's protective ability in magic. Can help with any matters of the heart, finding love, self-healing, and removing bad luck. Place roses on your love altar to honor Venus, goddess of love, beauty (and much more).

- **Skullcap.** Used in money magic, also used to keep partners (usually the masculine energy) faithful in relationships. Can also be helpful in fostering peacefulness. Some of this herb in a lover's shoe is used to help keep them from being noticed by others.

- **Wormwood.** It is said to be good for creating peace in war-like conditions. Also helpful in protection and assisting in receiving clairvoyant information. Can be carried or placed as protection from accidents, so in a satchel, bag, or car.

- **Yarrow.** Popular in spells and workings for courage and self-confidence. Useful for healing and drawing love to anyone who wears it in a sachet. Rubbing over your eyes is said to help with clairvoyance.

Waters

Beware of applying waters and the oils listed in the next section on your skin or ingesting them. I do not recommend you put any of these on your skin or eat them, you have to know what is safe for you.

- **Florida Water.** A widely popular in many magical practices, but hoodoo in particular. It is an all-purpose water that can be used across multiple purposes in your magic. Technically a cologne.

- Attract good spirits and repel negative ones.

    o   Cleanse your area before working by using it in a spray.

    o   Add to your ancestor altar as an offering.

    o   Create a wipe for your altar and use it for regular cleanings.

    o   Add to spiritual baths and scrubs. While Florida Water is considered safe for skin, you want to test this out first.

- ***Kananga Water.*** It is a cologne used for spiritual cleansing and protection in the same way as Florida Water, though not as widely available.

- ***Orange Water.*** Made with orange essential oil mixed in distilled water. Used topically for those who are wishing to increase their luck or looking to get married. Offer on money and love altars. Use it as a wash in a bath or shower. Can also be added to your altar when doing rituals or prayers focused on love or fortune.

- ***Peace Water.*** As the name suggests, used to promote peace wherever it is used. Comes in an indigo blue color. Use on self-love or altars for the home. Sprinkle around your space after cleaning to encourage a peaceful environment.

- ***Rose Water.*** Generally used on the body to attract love, also used in beautification rituals and spells. Can also be offered on love altars or to love goddesses. Add to baths and include it as an offering on your altar.

- ***War Water.*** Used in witch wars and for hexing. Often contains an iron nail along with herbs and plants consistent with the purpose. *Definitely* not for drinking.

- ***Willow Water.*** Like a tree that grows near water and is often found in or around graveyards (usually in the South), willow water is good for healing, poured as an offering at gravesites. It's considered a natural remedy to physical ailments and can be offered on ancestor altars. Can also be presented as an offering to your herbs, plants, and roots.

CHAPTER 6: DIRT IN HOODOO PRACTICES

According to the Loci, or "spirit of place," particular places are inhabited by spirits or deities that may be sought or appeased to fulfill our objectives and ambitions. It is currently largely regarded as the energy that inhabits a certain location in the contemporary period. This energy can be obtained in the form of dirt that occupies a certain location.

Hoodoo's Distribution of the Earth

Dirt/earth, like plants and dry powders, can be utilized in various ways. Personally, I spread the dirt on a level area and then make a symbol or write a keyword suggestive of my aim in it. I then address the individual whose grave the dirt was taken and solicit their assistance. Remember that when they received payment for the dirt, they committed to assisting. Following that, the dirt is collected and disseminated in various ways.

It might, for example, be placed in a fanny pack or mojo bag or folded into a parcel. It might be sprinkled on a dressed candle (the oil will make the dirt adhere to the candle, but don't use too much), a house or company, etc. In rare circumstances, the ghost whose grave the dirt is coming from will instruct you on using the dirt.

The Power of Dirt

Just like you wouldn't throw any plant inside of working without knowing what the plant is and why you're using it, you wouldn't collect and use dirt from just anywhere.

Especially not a graveyard.

As discussed in the section Working with Place, dirt from different locations can help with our magic. Aside from graveyards. Below are certain examples of where dirt can be gathered and what it can be used for. They are as follows:

- Bank - a financial institution that attracts and retains funds.

- Hospital - for health and healing.

- Police station - for protection

- Court - for success in legal proceedings.

- The church - for spiritual protection and collaboration with beneficial spiritual forces.

- Casino - for good fortune in gambling.

- Post Office - used for sending and receiving mails.

- Bordello / Sexy Shop - for desire, sex, and seduction spells

- Bookstore / Library - knowledge acquisition, school or college achievement

- Gymnasium - an achievement in athletics and sporting events

Folks definitely get creative when it comes to collecting dirt. Any place you come across has a spirit, and that spirit gets into the soil around and underneath. With the right process, you could technically collect dirt from anywhere, not just the ones listed above.

If you're in or around a major city, there's dirt from districts, like financial or fashion. You could potentially get dirt from a neighborhood, a beach, park, zoo, airport or bus terminal, community center, city hall, soccer or sports field, club, animal shelter, even an adult store.

There is dirt and dust used in hoodoo that doesn't come from a specific place but is tied to a circumstance or situation. One example is anvil dust, which is commonly substituted with magnetic dust in many spells. These two things are not the same.

Anvil dust is specifically collected from what is leftover in a blacksmith's shop, where hard work happens and direct focus is necessary. Anvil dust is infused with that spirit.

Taking dirt from a place is taking some of the power for your own purposes, so before going out to collect dirt, you want to know why you're taking dirt and what you plan to do with it.

You also want to take with you something to leave in place of whatever you took. Coins are a common offering, as is rum or whisky. If you don't want to leave anything or disturb the roots, you can clean up any garbage left in the area and leave the space better than you found it.

Collecting graveyard dirt isn't for the novice practitioner, but if you do venture out, you want to ensure to collect at the right time. Take note of the cycle of the moon and time of day. As a general guide, collecting after midnight and in the early morning hours is best.

Another consideration is the exact location of the dirt collected, again, this is especially true when collecting graveyard dirt. Depending on your spell, you may want to collect dirt underneath a shadow, at the entrance or the four corners of the graveyard.

In this case, it is definitely safer to purchase from someone who is more experienced at collecting graveyard dirt rather than collecting yourself. If you feel anything negative *at all*, leave the graveyard and do not collect any dirt.

Practitioners will also be sure to leave something in exchange for the dirt they collect.

Power Places

Places of power

As previously said, hoodoo practitioners believe that the energy of the cosmos is universal - that divine forces are all around us, ready to be harnessed via the proper channels. However, it should be mentioned that there are specific sites where the spiritual forces existing in the physical realm are more concentrated due to the hallowed character of these places or because of historical events that have occurred there. This part will look at some of these "power points" and how they relate to rituals and spellcasting procedures.

The Graveyard

Graveyard soil has previously been addressed several times in this work, demonstrating how strong the graveyard can be as a source of enormous spiritual power and energy, which, when channeled properly, may dramatically increase a person's magical skills. I make my way to the primordial plane. However, when their corpses degrade into the earth, remnants of their spiritual powers evaporate into the surrounding environment. The presence of several corpses rotting within the earth adds to the power of a graveyard's atmosphere. People can utilize graveyards and graves to take power from the surroundings and fuel their spells when performing a big spell that demands a lot of spiritual energy. The larger the graveyard or cemetery, the more power may be extracted from it in most circumstances. The grade of persons buried in a certain graveyard may likewise influence the quantity of power that may be harnessed from that type of location. A graveyard full of deceased witches and diviners may be a source of great power that can result in cataclysmic results when channeled by an equally strong diviner.

The Home

You might not believe it, but your house probably has more spiritual energy than you think. Residential structures, particularly those with a large number of occupants, may be huge repositories of distinct individual spiritual energy.

Compared to vacant buildings and commercial sites where people merely come and go, a person's house is an important place to them—and they perform the majority of their activities there—they sleep and wake up there, eat, freshen up, and entertain visitors. As you continue to leave in your ho, moi, you gradually deposit significant quantities of spiritual energy in there over time. When evil individuals reside in a house and infuse it with their bad energy, those energies may stay active long after the evil people die, transforming the house into a haven for evil and mischievous spirits.

As a result, your house may be an important site to perform rituals and make sacrifices to the spirits.

The Bank

In some cultures, money is said to be a spirit. Everyone wants money, and we all spend a significant portion of our lives attempting to obtain it. Banks may be extraordinarily effective centers of spiritual power due to the importance of money in people's lives and the heated spiritual energies surrounding money. Banks typically contain significant sums of money, making them ideal locations for casting spells to bring good fortune and wealth because of the abundance of spiritual energies associated with these beings in banks.

The Church

Hoodoo rituals and magic spells are often carried out in churches, even though this may appear strange or blasphemous to some, but churches are revered in hoodoo tradition as sacred sites of power. People visit churches to pray and connect with God. People begin to commit themselves to the service of the supernatural. Because the church is a place of worship for a higher force, it is a wonderful site of power. Aside from the unique type of contact that occurs within the four walls of a church, the huge number of people present in a church may also make it a location of extraordinary spiritual energy.

The Hospital

People visit hospitals to get treated for various ailments. Illnesses are expressions of a person's bad spiritual energy. Positive energies provide power, vitality, well-being, health, wealth, and vigor. On the other hand, negative energies are associated with illness, poverty, weakness, drowsiness, and, in the most extreme situations, death. Care must be taken when performing rituals and casting spells at a hospital. On the other hand, a hospital might be a supercharged place of negative energies associated with disease and death. However, power is power, whether bad or positive and when channeled properly, a hospital may be a wonderful environment to gain great spiritual powers.

Graveyard Dirt

Dirt and dust are different things. The dirt from graveyards is the actual soil surrounding the grave, while the dust is residual material found on the surface. The Bokongo people of Central Africa are believed to be the source of this form of magic, and they believed that the dirt contained the spirits of the people buried in the soil. When they traveled to America in 1730 as slaves, they brought this concept with them.

Graveyard dirt can't just be taken. It needs to be purchased. This involves communing with the dead person and creating a contract to buy the dirt. This would usually involve the purchaser leaving a gift on the grave for the deceased, usually in something they enjoyed in life, like liquor or money.

Not all graveyard dirt is equal. The dirt from the graves of babies and young children is especially powerful for healing and spells of good fortune, while the dirt from directly above the heart of the body is used for love spells. If you plan more iniquitous deeds, then the dirt from a murderer's grave will prove more powerful. Dirt from the graves of lesser criminals can be used to cast spells of chaos and disorder.

According to the Bokongo people of central Africa, cemetery dirt contains powerful magic. The dirt contains the spirit of the person buried there. Bokongo slaves brought this belief to the Americas in the 1730s.

You can't just take dirt from a cemetery; it must be bought. This involves communicating with the dead and offering them something in return for the dirt, often liquor or something they enjoyed in life. In the 19th century, the typical payment was a silver penny.

Not all cemetery dirt is created equal. Children's graves are sought after for blessings and good luck. Love spells are best performed with the dirt of someone who loved you, ideally the dirt that was on their heart. If you have evil in mind, the grave of a murderer is preferable. Minor criminals such as con men and tricksters have good dirt to cause mess and confusion.

When you consider that one of Hoodoo's primary factors is ancestral spirits, it should come as no surprise that you will also be working in graveyards. Now, working in graveyards is not exactly a beginner's tactic, but it is a key part of hoodoo. It requires a high degree of intuition and focus because there may be spirits there that are not pleased that you are there when you enter. They may not be there to help you, and that can become dangerous for you as well. Some spirits would prefer to be left alone or would prefer to lead you astray. As a beginner, it would be better for you to focus on your time at home. Learn to develop your skills with the ancestral altar and use it before you start delving into graveyards, which will be dangerous for you. Eventually, when you have got that spiritual intuition and that experience with your ancestors, you can start trying to experiment with graveyards, but do not do so lightly.

Before we delve further into discussing graveyards, however, remember that graveyards are not evil. They are not negative, either. They are actually, in hoodoo, believed to be highly revered. Rather than being places of grief and sadness, they are regarded as places of reverence. After all, in hoodoo, you are acknowledging that death is not final. Death is not the end of everything—rather, it is the beginning of the next phase. Your ancestors have died; they are no longer walking on this earth in their physical forms, but they still exist. They are still there, and their energy is still prevalent if you know where you are looking or what you need. If you can understand this concept, you start to step away from those negative connotations that the graveyard may initially evoke. Yes, you leave the bodies of your loved ones behind in them. However, their energy lives on.

We acknowledge that the graveyard becomes a place where we can access the energies of our loved ones. Death is a connection between our world and the next one, and because of that, the graveyard becomes symbolic of that journey.

The graveyard, then, creates the effect of evoking transitions. It is the beginning and the end at the same time. Graveyard earth can be that perfect way to harness the energy you need to represent that end or beginning. It can help to end eras or times. However, it can also be used to create new beginnings.

Remember, however, that when you take earth from a grave, you need to pay attention to where you are. You need to be selective of the people whose graves you take from. If you were to choose the wrong graves, you could end up creating issues with your spells. And, if you are not respectful, you can actually cause other problems as well.

Collecting graveyard dirt must be very respectful and almost even formal at times. You want to make sure that you are only to choose the right grave, paying attention to the energy that you wish to evoke, but you must also appease the spirit that resides there. It would help if you were respectful of their resting place and either pay for the soil with some pennies or with some whiskey or something else. This helps to show them that you are thanking them for the soil.

There are different ways that you can choose out a grave to draw from a spirit. From being able to figure out what the power of that spirit is through divination to using your own intuition after getting the experience necessary, you can start figuring out what you are doing with ease. Walk around the graveyard that you are in. Start taking the time to figure out what you are doing and get a feel for where you are. Get to know the spirits. You may find some that draw you, and if you do feel compelled to approach one, remember that you should do your research.

Remember that with this kind of magic, however, you are not just trying to get something. You are making relationships. You are building that connection with the energy of another being that was also once alive. You are not just trying to buy their services with a splash of whiskey or a few bites of something. You are trying to create that relationship to rely upon the people you are connected to.

Death in Hoodoo

Many Root Operators begin to work with the dead's spirits in the form of Ancestors, the spirits of the dead connected to them by blood. It is believed that the dead do not die but rather ascend to another level of being, from which they can watch over us and help us. From this higher level, the Ancestors can guide us in our daily life, intercede with the Divinity on our behalf and protect us in our time of need.

The process of working with the Ancestors begins with the construction of an Ancestral Altar. Before I go any further, I would like to point out that many of the rootworkers are Christians and adhere to God's commandment in Exodus 20:3 to "have no other gods before me." Therefore, the rootworkers do NOT worship the Ancestors because they worship them. The ancestral altar is the place where this veneration takes place ritually. (See also The Ancestors) In other cases, a practitioner may visit the cemetery to ritually collect dirt from a particular tomb or graves for use in spells and rituals. There are many variables to consider when collecting dirt from the cemetery for spells and rituals. Some of these variables include:

- Position of the grave

- How the person died

- Obtain permission

- Where to collect dirt

Moreover, the cemetery's dirt is not simply taken but rather paid for after negotiating with an appropriate spirit. Some practitioners regard work with the Saints and the Saints of the People as a form of work with the dead, since the Saints were once living human beings who also lived exceptionally virtuous lives.

What is Goofer Dust?

The name derives from the Bantu word kufua, which means "to die," and it is used to harm or kill the targeted victim. Composed primarily from graveyard dirt and dust, it also incorporates other ingredients depending on the required outcome. Snakeskin and salt are added to the dust to create a powerful way to cause someone harm.

The Goofer dust is spread on the victim's pillow or around the path they use to cause the greatest damage. The first sign the hex has worked is sharp pains in the legs or feet followed by severe swelling, which leads to the inability to walk. The term has also evolved to become a verb and a noun. The term "goofering someone" refers to any practice that involves a form of poisoning or inflicting harm by introducing injurious elements into their environment.

In January 2016, a man from Queens was sentenced to 50 years in prison for killing his parents five years earlier. After firing four sets of defense lawyers, he represented himself in court and claimed that his parents died as a direct result of his mother's use of goofer dust in the home. The truth was that he bludgeoned his mother to death and choked her with a pearl necklace before plunging her head into the bathtub.

Working with Place

Spirit is everywhere. Have you ever walked into a place and noticed that it just *felt* different? Some would call this a "vibe," short for vibration. You feel this when you walk into someone's home, but types of places have the same effect.

Think about what it feels like to walk into a school, a library, or a bodega. Each of these places has a distinct vibe to it that you know but don't think about too much.

Graveyards and crossroads are two important places in hoodoo because of the energy they carry. Other places that you'll often hear or read about in your research are banks and churches.

Specifically, you'll most often work with the spirit of a place like a bank by using the dirt from the land around where it is located (if it's surrounded by concrete, that is another story). You could really get creative with this, but using dirt from just anywhere could produce unintended results.

The symbolism of crossroads is also big in conjure. The crossroads represent many things. In our plane of existence, we live in a world where we can experience both 3D life and the spirit world.

CHAPTER 7: MAGIC CANDLES

As you begin your hoodoo work, you'll quickly discover the importance of candles. When it comes to depicting magick, this is one of the things Hollywood gets right.

Your first hoodoo candle will probably be called a 7-day candle. These are available in a tall, glass cylinder, and as their name suggests, are built to last seven days. They are about 8 inches high and just over 2 inches in diameter.

You may have seen religious 7-day candles before. These are the ones with religious figures depicted on them, like Mother Mary, and may have a prayer printed on the back.

You can get plain candles or ones in various colors. A 7-day candle may have seven different colors or two. These different colors can help you with blessing your candle, and with doing spells that require you to do a working every day for a week.

Some spells require you to bless a candle halfway up and halfway down. Two-colored 7-day candles show you easily where the halfway mark is.

One kind of candle you can purchase can have multiple colors, sometimes two, but you can find candles with up to seven colors in a column as if each color is stacked one on another.

Another type of candle that is easier to use for spells and is not designed to last more than a week is the smaller, thinner pillar in different colors. You could make these candles stand on something by melting the wax at the bottom and sticking the candle down on whatever you're working on.

Using a Lamp

In addition to candles, part of your practice can include the use of hoodoo lamps. If you have a traditional lamp at home, consider yourself lucky. You can use these lamps in your hoodoo.

More often, you'll find the kind of lamp that is created using a mason jar or other glass-type of container. Most of your magical items and ingredients will go inside of the jar with your oil. Your floating wick would then go on top of the oil, and you can light it to activate your lamp.

What you're creating will look different from anything you may have seen in the past. Even in the hoodoo tradition, there aren't many people who create lamps. That said, it is not complicated.

At the end of your working, you'll most likely have your lamp sitting on a plate with different curios and items floating inside of the glass, with your flame or wick burning on top. On the plate, you may have more curios or items with the purpose of bolstering your work.

Generally, these floating wicks can last up to 24 hours, but you never want to leave an open flame by itself.

The Candle Materials

Of course, as mentioned above, the best candles of all are those that the magician makes himself using pure beeswax. This is basically for two reasons:

The first is that the operator can infuse (consciously or unconsciously) his energy during the various stages of the process. The second reason is that virgin wax is a natural, living material that vibrates with light energy (it is no coincidence that bees have always been considered "solar" creatures).

These considerations make "self-made" candles more effective in their function of channeling astral energies. Furthermore, when we need to get rid of the remnants of a ritual, we can easily (e.g.) bury the remaining wax because, as beeswax is natural and biodegradable, we can be sure that its dispersion in the environment will be more respectful towards Mother Earth.

However, many people find it inconvenient to make their own candles. In fact, it is a question of finding good quality wax, suitable wicks, molds, the right melting temperature, cooling and extraction from the molds, *etc.* There is a risk that you will find yourself in a situation where you have to make your own candles. There is a risk of finding something that should look like a candle but in the end, does not burn properly. Good results require a certain amount of practice and effort.

A good alternative is that there are ready-made candles made of pure beeswax on the market... the practitioner simply has to purify them and charge them with his personal energy before performing any magic ritual. Obviously, the color of these candles is golden yellow (solar) or white (if the beeswax has been bleached). These are "universal" colors, so they are suitable for all sorts of rituals.

However, for those who prefer differently colored candles (in order to make the most of the subtle vibration of the colors), there are excellent candles available on the market made of pure vegetable stearin from coconut palms, dyed with food coloring. These candles are also fully biodegradable and therefore respect the natural balance.

As a last choice, there are regular candles made of non-biodegradable stearin. The qualities of these are very variable, certainly inferior to the natural and biodegradable candles seen above. In general, we can say that the price is a good indicator of the quality of a candle. In fact, the more expensive the candle, the better (from both a magical and a natural point of view) the materials used in its manufacture.

Burning candles in magic

We usually think of candles as something that, once lit, has a fixed duration. In fact, in the boxes of commercial candles, there is an indication of the burning time (e.g., "duration 8 hours"). In reality, the indication is a kind of "average" since a candle can burn faster or slower depending on the case.

In any case, the slowness or rapidity with which candles are consumed in the context of a magic ritual is of considerable importance. In general, we can say that if a candle is consumed rapidly in a spell, it is a sign that in the Air present in the place or room in which we are operating, there will be a good quantity of Spirit Ether.

Vice versa, there will be little Astral Spirit in the Air if the candles are consumed more slowly than usual. The presence or absence of Spirit in the air depends on many factors, the most important of which are: astrological moment, geographical position, energies of the place where we operate, energies of the people or entities nearby, our state of mind, and last but not least, the type of rite or spell we are performing.

So if we are performing a constructive (or "white magic") spell, a fast-burning of the candles will be a good sign. It follows that our occult operation has an excellent chance of succeeding. Conversely, if the candles burn slowly, there is little chance that the ritual will be successful.

The opposite is true for destructive (or "black magic") rituals. Therefore, in the latter case, rapid combustion is a sign of vitality and a negative outcome of the ritual, while slow combustion indicates a positive outcome of the magical operation. Naturally, these are signs that provide general indications. Only time (and objective verification) will be able to say with absolute certainty whether an operation has been truly effective.

Preparing the Consecrated Oil

The candles should be "dressed," as we will see later. Generally, purified and consecrated oil is used for this operation. You can buy bottles of ready-to-use oil in various shops and esoteric bookshops but, as always, the best results are obtained by creating the oil yourself (and you save a lot of money in the process). So how do you do it?

Take a small bottle and put some extra virgin olive oil in it. Add a pinch of salt and, if you wish, other ingredients (herbs, essential oils) that match your purposes. For example, if you are going to do a ritual to attract money and abundance, you could add some dried apple seeds, orange juice, chamomile (open a bag of ordinary infusion and use a pinch of powder, or crumble some flowers, or use some essential oil to that aroma), *etc.* When you are satisfied and you have added all the ingredients you consider useful, place the bottle in a bain-marie in a small saucepan and heat it slightly. Caution: it should not boil but simply receive heat energy.

While the oil is heating up, consecrate it with your intention. There are, of course, many different methods (each Wizard or Witch develops in the course of their practice their own systems for consecrating ceremonial objects and instruments). Here is a fairly simple and complete one that you can use or modify as you wish.

Draw with the index finger of your right hand (with the Wand or the Athame) a Pentagram of Invocation (depending on the purpose, the symbol can refer to a different Element. For example, you can use an Earth invocation staff following the example above, as it is the Element most directly connected with money and prosperity).

Then place your right hand over the bottle at a distance that allows you to feel the heat without burning yourself, and recite a consecration formula. Below, you can read some of them, just as an example:

Creator Spirit, descend into this oil and consecrate it with your virtue. Let every spirit, ghost, larva and evil shadow be cast out of it, and let every lie and illusion be banished. Make it sacred and pure so that I may use it for my Work. With the blessing of all, without harm to any, so be it.

Those who have more affinity with the Judeo-Christian tradition can recite some passages from the Bible, for example:

Then Moses took the anointing oil, anointed the dwelling and all things therein, and so consecrated them.

(Leviticus 8: 10)

Or the formula for anointing the Oil of Catechumens, used during baptism (when you see the symbol "+", make a sign of the cross with the index finger of your right hand, the Wand or the Athame, on the oil that is being heated):

Ego te linio + Oleo salutis in Christo + Jesu Domino nostro + Ut habeas vitam aeternam, Amen + Or the formula used for the consecration of Chrism in Catholic ceremonies:

Lord, bless this oil, so that you may infuse into it the power of the Holy Spirit with which you united the priests, kings, prophets and martyrs.

Continuing the example of the ritual about money and prosperity, the deities most closely related to such an intention could be Hermes/Mercury, Ganesh, Lakshmi, Abundantia, Plutus, Horus, Renenutet, Anuket, Teutates (Toutatis), Odino/Wotan. In addition, you could invoke the spirit of the Archangel Metatron or Uriel (linked to the North, the fertile land and its fruits), as well as various Spirits and Demons of Goetia who deal specifically with attracting money and wealth. Staying with the classic, a possible invocation to Hermes/Mercury for this ritual could be the following:

I call the Messenger of the Holy Gods

Faster than the wind

Faster than the thunderbolts of Zeus

Angelos Athanaton

Come ratting with winged feet

I call the lord of cunning

Mechaniotes

God of serpents

Who guides the path of Psyche

Through heavenly and chthonic gates

In life and in death

In dreaming and waking

I call on him to whom no path is hidden

Remove every obstacle in my path

Sanctify this oil dedicated to you

Bring me your gifts, Holy Hermes

So be it!

If we choose to use this formula, it might be a good idea to do the oil consecration ritual on a Wednesday, possibly in the hour of Mercury or Jupiter.

Dressing the Candles

Take the candle with your left hand (the receptive hand) and wet the fingers of your right hand (the projective hand) with the consecrated oil (remember, wait until it has cooled down).

The Moon Phases

- The New Moon or also Black Moon is in tune with the purification rites, amplifies the effect in the period of the lunation, and influences the actions performed on the day of the new moon.

- The Crescent Moon lasts about two weeks, the lunar energy increases the vital force and the earth's magnetism: these are good days for rituals related to actions that need to be carried out quickly.

- The Full Moon is the most suitable and most important phase for oneself since it is the complete maturation of what has been conceived and developed during the phases of the New Moon and the Crescent Moon.

- The Waning Moon can be used to reverse a health problem, to remove obstacles, to silence gossip. It is the ideal time to maintain lasting results.

Days of the Week for Candle Magic

Depending on the wish, we have to choose the right day of the week, matching the planets, colors, essential oils, incense, and zodiac signs.

Monday: Day of the Moon

- Zodiac sign: Cancer
- Candle color: White - Light blue - Pastel green
- Essential oils: Sandalwood - Jasmine
- Incense: Sandalwood - Ginger - Jasmine.

Tuesday: Day of Mars

- Zodiac signs: Aries - Scorpio
- Color: Red - Bordeaux
- Essential oils: Pepper - Thyme - Hot pepper
- Incense: Black pepper - Geranium - Nettle

Wednesday: Mercury Day

- Zodiac signs: Gemini - Virgo
- Color: Light Yellow - Dark Green - Light Brown - Copper
- Essential oils: Aniseed - Cumin - Fennel
- Incense: Cinnamon - Lavender - Chamomile

Thursday: Day of Jupiter

- Zodiac signs: Sagittarius - Pisces

- Color: Blue - Turquoise - Violet

- Essential oils: Cedar - Nutmeg

- Incense: Cedar - Mint - Benzoin - Saffron

Friday: Day of Venus

- Zodiac signs: Taurus - Libra

- Color: Green - Pink

- Essential oils: Myrtle - Rose - Vervain

- Incense: Rose - Orange Blossom - Apple

Saturday: Day of Saturn

- Zodiac signs: Capricorn - Aquarius

- Color: Olive Green - Dark Brown - Black

- Essential oils: Cypress

- Incense: Myrrh - Musk - Dandelion

Sunday: The day of the Sun

- Sign of the Zodiac: Leo

- Color: Gold - Yellow - Orange - Silver

- Essential oils: Orange - Cinnamon

- Incenses: Olibanum - Saffron - Laurel

Colors and Signs of the Zodiac

- Aries - red

- Taurus - green

- Gemini - yellow

- Cancer - silver

- Leo - orange/gold

- Virgo - brown

- Libra - pink

- Scorpio - black

- Sagittarius - purple

- Capricorn - blue

- Aquarius - white

- Pisces - purple

CHAPTER 8: MAGIC OILS

Oils are another curious part of a religion that has been used throughout the ages. You will find the use of oils in virtually all religions. In Hoodoo, oils are used as an accelerant and a sealant. In other words, when you put a specific oil on an object or place, or person, you are accelerating the power of the spell that you want to invoke or conjure within that object, place, or person. You can also use it to seal that power that has been placed in/on them. For example, if you consecrate a specific place and assign it as holy, you need an oil to seal this consecration process. So whatever kind of spell you want to create, there is an oil mixture that can aid that process, and that is what we'll talk about in this chapter. I will share the core uses of oil in Hoodoo and then highlight a spell that utilizes oils in its enchantment.

Understanding Magic Powder and Oils

Powders and oils are an integral part of the Hoodoo tradition. They have been used for centuries, long before it became commonplace to use essential oils for aromatherapy. The only difference between the general use of oils and the way they are used in Hoodoo practices is that each oil is conditioned with a purpose. This tradition is perhaps what gave rise to the knowledge that certain scents are associated with certain emotions and can invoke certain feelings. For example, the scent of citrus is said to inspire creativity. There is a lot of science that backs up the effectiveness of these aromatherapy oils. But as you well know by now, Hoodoo is not exactly science that can be cooked up in a laboratory. It requires the merging of mind and spirit.

Oils and powders are extracted from plants, and so, with the understanding of plant spirits and what they represent, you can extract the essence of that plant, combine it with other herbs in specific portions, and then bind that to a purpose with your mind. It really is as simple as that. However, the process is very delicate. Some oils and powders have been crafted for this particular purpose.

While there are many experts and people like myself who are deeply steeped in the practice of Hoodoo who can create the right oils for you, there is something beautiful about being able to create a unique mix for you. Eventually, as you advance and grow in the craft, you might be able to create these mixtures for other people as well. My goal and desire here are to pass on my knowledge to create your herb mixes, oils, and potions that are just as effective as mine, if not more so because they are specific to you. To create your own oil and powder mix, the first place to start is to understand plants. Now you see why I said it is essential to research all these herbs and plants. Don't just focus on their magical properties. You have to identify them individually. There are different species of each plant, which are unique to their geographical location. Mastering their uses and extraction process requires constant practice and study.

Conjure Oils

Conjure oils and incantations from a time when life was closer to the earth. Hoodoo is one of the most misunderstood practices in witchcraft, or perhaps witchcraft is misunderstood in how it relates to Hoodoo. In either case, there are many misconceptions about what this practice entails and who its practitioners are.

Hoodoo practitioners were once primarily male, but more women are involved today than ever before. While their numbers have decreased, they still remain a minority within the broader world of witchcraft.

Hoodoo practitioners (or practitioners of hoodoo) generally work with herbs, roots and other plants in combination with more complex and elaborate spells. Though there are many similarities between hoodoo and other forms of witchcraft, there are also differences that set hoodoo apart from them as well.

Hoodoo consists of a set of practices that are derived from African cultural and spiritual traditions. Most hoodoo practitioners are also practitioners of more mainstream witchcraft, like Wicca or ceremonial magic. In fact, hoodoo was the ancestor of these forms of witchcraft as well as other magical systems that developed later in the New World like Santeria and Voodoo.

There are several unique aspects to hoodoo, including some practices that are frowned upon by many other forms of witchcraft. The use of eggs in spells, for example, is something not practiced by many Wiccans - but it's common in hoodoo. That said, there are also similarities between hoodoo and other forms of witchcraft as well.

How to Use Conjure Oils

The potency of a powder like this depends on how well it latches on to that person's imprint, which carries their essence. You will quickly learn about Hoodoo magic because the essence of a person is an important ingredient in increasing the potency of the spell you are casting. This is because the spell in question is no longer generic but has a unique identity to work with. Let us say you live in a neighborhood that is relatively quiet, except for one annoying neighbor who is a nuisance to you. A quick way to get them out of your life without having to tip the balance of good and evil is to use Hoodoo powder. Sprinkle this powder on a well-known path where they walk. Mixing the powder with a little bit of dirt will help disguise it. Once you have sprinkled it, you have to seal the spell with your intention by vocally saying their name and what you want to happen. There are specific powder mixtures that can act as a repellent, and when you attach your intention to such a mixture, you are guaranteed to get results almost immediately. This can also work if you are trying to get attention from that person.

Oils work a little differently from powders, which has a lot to do with their consistency. For instance, if you sprinkle oil on an invoice, it would look tacky, and you would come off as unprofessional. This bad impression that the image creates will set the mind of the recipient against you. So it is better to use powder in certain situations and oils in others. One instance where both oil and powders can be used is when you are creating a spell or working with candle magic. There are candles that are created for spell purposes. Sprinkle a little bit of powder or oil on the uppermost part of the area where the candle is burning and then place your intentions on that candle so that as it burns, the spell will be activated and cause your desires to manifest in your life. You can also use oils and powders as a way to feed your mojo bags. In the next chapter, we are going to be talking in greater detail about mojo bags. But the thing you need to understand about them right now is that their power wanes over time. For this reason, you need powders and oils to continue feeding that energy if you want to keep the spell active and relevant.

There are many other ways to use Hoodoo oils and powders, but I am saving some of those tips for the chapters where we get into the creation of spells, so you can see this part of Hoodoo practice in action. For now, the only thing left to discuss is how to create or conjure up your own magic oils and powders.

Oils and Potions

This heading delves into some of the most popular oils and potions used in Voodoo hoodoo. You would either need to discover how to create them or buy them for several of the spells. Most conventional rootworkers create their own, but technological advancements and internet connections have made it simpler for some people to buy what they need. You are free to choose whatever you desire; there is no rule requiring you to create your own. Making your own has the bonus of knowing just what's in it and being able to charge it yourself.

Carrier Oils

Grapeseed Oil has a shelf life of around 3-6 months. Grapeseed oil processed with solvents has a 9-month shelf life. Keep refrigerated until ready to use.

Abyssinian Seed Oil - Mustard Seed - Shelf life is roughly about 18 to 24 months.

Olive oil has a shelf life of 12 to 18 months if properly stored in a cold, dark place.

If not refrigerated, sweet almond oil has a shelf life of around 3-6 months. The shelf life can be extended to 12 months if refrigerated.

Precautionary Measures

Please keep in mind that any oil or oil mix may cause an allergic reaction. Until using any essential oil that can come into contact with the skin, a skin patch examination should be performed. This is to see if you're allergic to the oil or if you have a sensitization reflex to it.

1) Keep all oils out of the reach of children and pets.

2) Pregnant women and people with health issues should seek medical advice.

3) Essential oils should never be applied to the skin undiluted.

4) Essential oils can never be consumed.

5) Natural ingredient-based products can also induce allergic reactions in certain people.

Working with essential oils necessitates knowledge of the oils' properties and awareness of the oils' safety concerns.

- ***Hazardous Oils:*** Bitter Almond, Elecampane, Arnica, Costus, Boldo, Cinnamon (bark), Broom, Chervil, Buchu, Camphor, Calamus, Cassia, Fennel(bitter), Wormseed, Horseradish, Tonka, Mugwort, Thuja, Mustard, Tansy, Oregano, Savory, Pennyroyal, Sage (common), Sassafras, Santolina, Savine, Wintergreen, and Wormwood are some of the Hazardous oils.

- ***Toxicity:*** Essential oils such as Ajowan, Sage (exotic), Anise Star, Pepper (black), Basil (exotic), Parsley, Bay Laurel, Nutmeg, Bay (West Indian), Juniper, Camphor (white), Fennel (sweet), Cassie, Cedarwood (Virginian), Hyssop, Cinnamon (leaf), Hops, Clove (bud), Fennel (sweet), Eucalyptus, Coriander, should be used in moderation.

- ***Dermal Irritation:*** Ajowan, Thyme (white) Allspice, Peppermint, Aniseed, Parsley, Basil (sweet), Lemon, Garlic, black pepper, Ginger, Boreal, Eucalyptus, Cajeput, Cornmint, Caraway, Clove (bud), Cinnamon (leaf), Cedarwood (Virginian), and Turmeric are some of the Oils that can irritate the skin, particularly when used in high concentrations.

- ***Sensitization:*** Certain oils can irritate the skin only in people with extremely sensitive skin or cause an allergy in some people. Before using fresh oil, always do a thorough inspection to ensure that you are not allergic to it. Basil (French), Pine (Scotch and long-leaf), Bay Laurel, Peru Balsam, Benzoin, Orange, Cade, Mint, Mastic, Lovage, Canagaa, Litsea Cubeba, Cedarwood (Virginian), Lemon Balm (melissa), Lemongrass, Lemon, Chamomile (Roman and German), Jasmine, Citronella, Geranium, Garlic, Hops, Ginger, and Styrax are some of the oils that can cause irritation to some people.

- ***Phototoxicity:*** Certain oils are phototoxic, which means that they can induce skin pigmentation if exposed to direct sunlight. If the region may be exposed to the light, do not use the below oils on the skin, either pure or in dilution: Angelica Root, Lovage, Bergamot (except bergapten-free type), Lime (expressed), Ginger, Cumin, Lemon (expressed), Mandarin, Verbena. and Orange.

- ***High Blood Pressure:*** Hyssop, Sage (Spanish and Common), Rosemary, and Thyme are all oils to avoid if you have high blood pressure.

- ***Epilepsy:*** Fennel (sweet).

- ***Diabetes:*** Hyssop, Angelica, Rosemary, and Sage (all types).

- ***Homeopathy:*** Black pepper, eucalyptus, camphor, and peppermint are incompatible with homeopathic therapy.

Storage

Essential oils should be kept in dark glass bottles or vials to keep them fresh. On the other hand, critical oils can be wrapped in transparent glass bottles or vials and placed in a jar or dark carrying case. Keep all essential oils away from children and pets at a mild to cool temperature.

Formulas

Any of the formulas below will have detailed blending instructions, while others will not. Some people like the intensity of a specific herb or fragrance to vary based on the job or intent they are working on, so they change it accordingly. You can do it, too, because you've mastered both the mixing process and the properties of essential oils.

Meanwhile, below are some general instructions to follow when exact measures for a calculation are not provided.

- ***Anointing Oil*** - Various ratios of essential oils should be used to make anointing oils. To 1 oz. of carrier oil, add 60-75 drops of essential oil or essential oil mix.

- ***Spray*** – Fill an 8 oz. spray bottle with 30-50 drops of essential oil or essential oil mix. Fill the bottle of purified water to the top. The majority of spray bottles of this size will be plastic; however, keep in mind that the oils will eventually erode the plastic container.

- ***Bath Oil*** – To one ounce of carrier oil, add 5-7 drops of essential oils or an essential oil mix. Fill a pool of running water with a minimal volume of the mix. Before entering the bath, mix the water and oil.

Cleansing Oils

There are *many* different types of oils in the hoodoo practice. We're just going to list the cleansing oils here, but there is an oil for money and abundance, keeping your home peaceful, attracting love to you, hexing and blessing, breaking curses, and getting lucky.

To use the oils, you can anoint yourself anoint any special paperwork you're using for working or just in your life. You can anoint your altar or tools used on your altar, such as statues of deities. You can also use oils to bless your personal items, such as a wallet.

For this section of the book, we'll focus on just the oils for cleansing. As we'll cover in future chapters, cleansing and protection are very important when you're working with spirit.

- ***Cut & Clear.*** An oil you'll find at almost any hoodoo shop. For cutting and clearing anything out of your life, such as habits, exes, and attachments. Anoint yourself, use in personal care products, wear on your body like a perfume.

- ***Dragon's Blood.*** Considered a powerful all-purpose oil. It is red in color from Dragon's Blood, a deeply red-colored resin. Add some drops to your cleaning products or use them to anoint your tools and altar.

- ***Hindu Grass.*** An oil for cutting out things from your life. This could be a relationship or a pattern of thinking or behavior, tied to past events. An oil you can use on yourself, anointing and wearing.

- ***Blessing.*** There's Blessing oil *and* House Blessing oil. The first type is generally used for yourself, the second strictly for your home. These oils cleanse and are said to help bring favor from deities. Depending on the type of oil, you can use it on yourself or for your home. You could also offer this oil to your ancestors or deities you're working with by leaving some drops on a plate or leaving an open jar on your altar.

- ***Psychic Cleansing.*** If you need a psychic cleansing of old energies weighing you down or getting in your way, try a psychic cleansing oil. Anoint yourself before meditating or offer some of the oil on a self-love altar.

- ***Purification.*** A blaster of any blocks or energies that remain in your way. Not as available as the other oils, but an excellent option if you're just getting out of a bad relationship or attachment. Burn this oil on a charcoal disc or add it to a self-healing mojo bag.

Creating Personalized Oils

Creating your own oils will require having a neutral carrier oil as your base. Personally, I like to use homemade coconut oil. It is a very receptive oil and adapts its structure to whatever herbal elements you put in it. If you add very strong herbs, it will adjust its physiological nature and adopt the potency of whatever you are using. It is also soft enough to be flexible when you want something very mild. For love potions, I prefer to use oils extracted from flowers, like roses. The nature of the rose plant is very open to love, and when used in a spell, it can invoke very strong imagery in the mind of the recipients. As a beginner, I would recommend the oils I have listed below. When you become stronger in the craft, you can move on to oils like bergamot oil. For your first lesson, the intention is to create a ***"Get me a Job"*** oil. These are hard times we live in, and you might need a little spiritual boost to help you get ahead. For this oil, you will need the following:

- Allspice - Used in prosperity spells

- Cinnamon - Attracts luck

- Coconut oil - An excellent base oil

- Dill - To make you irresistible

- Sage - For wisdom and to ward off evil eyes

Use a transparent glass bottle for this work. Pour your base into this bottle or jar and then add the cinnamon, allspice, dill and sage. If you are using fresh dill and sage, you will need to prep them ahead of time by bruising the leaves a little before immersing them in oil. Let them sit in the bottle overnight, and then pour the oil and herb mixture into a strainer. Squeeze to extract and then use what is in the container. Ensure that no fresh leaves get into the mixture. Repeat this for three days with new dill and sage leaves.

On the third day, you should have enough to use for the mixture. Put the allspice and cinnamon into the oil/herb mixture. Shake it and set it down for an entire day. For the next week, continue shaking it several times every day. At the end of the seventh day, you have your first magic oil. Rub this on the sole of your shoe before you go for a job interview. You are bound to get positive outcomes. Another way to amplify the potency of this oil is to use it on a candle.

CHAPTER 9: ALTAR

Where in the use of European magic, the altar is a single, consecrated artifact, in hoodoo we speak more correctly of altars in the plural because the conjure man often has more than one. So there will be special altars depending on the technique used, the 'action, dedicated to more than one function and can be fixed or temporary. Usually, the altar is not consecrated in the true sense of the word and acquires power only by virtue of what is grouped there. The simplest thing is to give some practical examples. An altar for love will be dominated by the colors red and pink, there will be on it simple red candles or shaped like a phallus or vagina, sexual symbols, depictions of genitals, magnetic stones paired and loaded with magnetic powder, depictions of hearts, violets, roots of John the conqueror, images of saints related to love as St. Valentine or gods like Shiva and Parvati depicted in sexual union, oils and dust for luck in love and sex etc..

An altar for money and play will have a green color, will contain dice, green candles, symbols of $ and €, single magnetic stones, coins (especially leap years), teeth and legs of alligator or rabbit, chestnut chestnuts, dust and oils for luck and money, playing cards, horseshoes, depictions of Chinese fortune gods, lottery tickets with special numerical combinations, etc.

Finally, an altar dedicated to the curse will have a black look, will contain pepper and chili powder, curse oils, goofer dust, representations of the devil, black cats, pins, nails, rag dolls, black candles, bones, cemetery land, depictions of Baron Samedi and Maman Brigitte, Kali, etc.

Usually, rather than having a "handyman" altar (which is also possible and in some cases very practical), it is preferable to undo an altar that is no longer needed and redo an altar that is needed at the moment. Having a "handyman" altar would confuse the situation, and perhaps even the spirits, as well as having to be of considerable size to contain all the suitable objects.

Working Altars

An ancestor altar is very common in hoodoo practice. In addition to this, you may want to create an altar specifically for a certain aspect of your life or something you want.

Here, I go over a few of these types of altars and some ways you can get creative. With each, you want to think about how you can invite the presence of God and/or the Goddess (or Solar Light, whichever deity speaks to you). Your ancestor altar may have God in every aspect. Or you may use a candle to represent Solar Light.

Some altars are permanent, but if there's something specific you're working on, you could use a temporary altar.

The Self-Love Altar

If you've struggled with self-image issues or come from a childhood home where you witnessed violence, a self-love altar is a space to center and heal.

It's a place where you can take everything you love about yourself and honor it. This might require some creativity as you're taking intangible aspects and making them physical.

The four elements are thought to stand in for aspects of life and living: earth honors your foundation, water your emotions and intuition, wind your thinking, and fire your willpower. These are common elements in all altars. You can use things that you like to represent these elements.

For example, if you love frogs, you could create a self-love altar that is heavy on the frog decor. If you're an artist, you could paint your self-love altar on a massive canvas. The advantage of this is it saves space in your home.

Small statues, trinkets, and figurines are great for altars in general, but especially for tapping into your personality and attributes. Animal and mystical symbolism is great for this. A horse, for example, could represent freedom, strength of spirit, triumph, and courage. A fairy could represent a sense of wonder and magic.

A trinket like a pair of glasses or binoculars could represent foresight. Jewelry, abundance and beauty. Crystals like rose quartz are great to represent love.

A figurine of a small Oscar award can be immensely powerful if you one day want to win an Oscar.

As you can tell, the possibilities for this kind of altar are endless. Searching options on Google is a great option, but you can also use tarot cards or think of things that just mean something to you. However, don't deny the power in common symbols, like stars. Many times, you can go to a local dollar store and find lots of usable stuff. Or you may already have something at home.

You are a strong spirit. A self-love altar is a space where you can honor your true spirit, regardless of how you've had to shift and bend to exist in the world.

The Money Altar

What's your relationship with money? How do you feel when you look at people who have more money than you? A money altar is a space to heal your relationship with money if you need to or honor the strong relationship you already have.

Many of us have the misperception that "no one will pay us the money we want". A money altar is an ideal place to heal this idea.

You can be creative with this altar, creativity is the channel through which money and abundance flow. The only rule is to keep the intent of the altar focused. Putting a random object on your money altar will muddy up the lines of communication.

Money is one of the first things you want on this type of altar. If you have any dollar bills or coins hanging around, especially if they're different denominations, use these. It doesn't matter how much or what denomination you have, even monopoly money will work if you want it to.

Old checks hanging around are *great* for a money altar. This is an idea from The Secret but it applies here. You might have a check from a closed bank account. Use these to start writing checks to yourself with amounts that you want. Write an infinity check!

The usual items for most altars apply for this type as well: crystals, candles, herbs, roots, and other items like money, oils, and dirt that we have and will cover.

Statues of deities that are associated with wealth and money are ideal for a money altar, for example, Oshun, or Fortuna.

Tarot cards work as well, though you may want to purchase a deck that is separate from the one you use for readings, or you can print out an image online.

You want to think about things that mean something to you for your money altar. A growing plant can be a symbol of expansion. Watering a plant on your money altar every day can be important symbolism, same with pruning the plant and removing dead leaves (removing old ideas).

Pinecones or double samaras (those things that fall from trees in a pinwheel motion) are a symbol of abundance if you live in an area where these things are everywhere.

The Deity Altar

If you respect more than one deity, then you'll know whether you can use one altar for every deity or if you need one altar for each deity.

Some deities require their own space, so sharing their sacred space in your home is not an option.

You'll also want to know what the deity you're honoring likes to receive. Money is one example. It means something to us, and can work on your money altar, but some deities may not care for money at all.

One of the basics you'll want on the altar is a statue or some representation of the deity that the altar is being built for. Some altars will even include more than one statue or depiction. *You want these visual elements to represent the deity for you, items that as soon as you come into contact with them, you connect with your deity.*

Building Your Altar

How great is it to know that all of your problems can be solved with the help of the Spirit?

If you're beginning to feel some gratitude in knowing this, try to bottle up this feeling. Gratitude is the vibration you want to conjure and maintain when building your altar.

An altar is the physical manifestation of your relationship with your ancestors and a non-negotiable for the serious hoodoo practitioner.

This is a place for you to speak to and receive messages from your ancestors, a place to present your offerings and to do your work. It is a kind of a spiritual center for your home. You can also keep specific types of altars in your space for your work.

Some practitioners have multiple altars; they keep one specifically for their ancestors, another for working (which we'll get into later). An altar for money, one for love, the list goes on.

Do not worry if you don't have the space for all of this. The point is to have a dedicated area for your work. Altars can take different forms, but a basic altar set up usually has:

- A bible

- At least one candle

- Water in a wine glass or other glass

- Images of your ancestors

- Items belonging to your ancestors, such as jewelry

Usually, this is set up with a white tablecloth atop a table. You will find altars as different and varied as there are homes.

Other basics include food. This is usually cooked or baked, it's always better if you know what foods your ancestors preferred and take the time to prepare and offer what you know they like. You can also include your tarot cards or anything you use for divination, images, or any depictions you have of deities that mean something to you.

You don't want to keep food on your altar for too long. When drinks or food get cold, dispose of it. If you were to offer your ancestors an afternoon cup of tea, for example, in the evening, you dispose of it at your front door. Or, if you don't want to make a mess of your hallway, find a tree and pour it out there. This is how you dispose of food left on your altar as well; never throw out or put food in the compost.

Offerings can be left as often as you like, but try to ritualize this, for example leaving food once a week.

The table in your home can take any form. It might be built-in, like by a bay window or shelf. If you have more space, you can go bigger and use a small desk or table that has a dedicated spot in your home.

It's most important to set up an altar that works for you. This might mean creating an altar that doesn't *appear* like one at first glance. Or it might mean that you use a smaller table that can fit perfectly in a corner.

This space is and will become sacred. It should be out of the way of anyone touching it, other than you. Do not feel obligated to tell anyone what it is or why any of the items are on it. If it seems too many people are interacting with the space, you may want to move it to somewhere more private.

Once the altar is built, do a small ritual where you call on your ancestors. The main purpose of this is to present your altar space to them so that they know this is their physical home in your life, a representation of the home they have in your heart and mind.

Getting Prepared

You need a way to get calm and centered. Not just for this ritual, but for everything. You do not want to begin this ritual with *any* anxiety at all. Maybe you've never done this before, but remove any jitters or feelings of being 'freaked out.' Unsure is fine, but try to convert that unsure feeling to reverence.

Do something that tells your mind this is a special moment. One simple way to do this is to get dressed up; wear all white or something that marks what you're doing.

Prepare what you are going to present as offerings to your ancestors. A few ideas: coins, warm food, a drink you know they liked (though wine, rum, or whiskey will suffice), fresh flowers, coffee or tea (with sugar), coins, bread or fruit that has been cut and is ready to eat. If you leave food, like nuts or seeds, leave it open (i.e., not in a bottle or jar that's closed).

The last thing you want to have on hand is your prayers and a bible, either physical or digital to read from (unless you have what you want to recite memorized).

Your prayers will require some thought beforehand, depending on how formal you want to be. If you're more comfortable just talking to your ancestors like a friend, do that.

Opening the Ritual

Open the ritual by anointing yourself and your space with hoodoo oil. There are many ways to anoint yourself, but here's a simple method using your body's pressure points and third eye.

Set your intention (i.e., Say aloud something like: *Thank you, [your name for God] for facilitating my connection to my ancestors*.). Continue to repeat your intention throughout as you apply oil to your pressure points:

Apply a drop of the oil to one wrist and rub your wrists together, then apply oil (take more as needed):

- The upper shell of your ear.

- Behind your shoulders.

- Your third eye.

Alternatively, if you don't have an oil or prefer not to use them on your skin, you can anoint with a spray or a cologne.

Do not worry about buying an oil or spray. These can be made with water and a few ingredients you probably already have in your kitchen. These instructions will be covered in Part 2, under Cleaning Rituals and Spirit Washes.

With sprays, you set and state your intention while spraying the air at least once. Three times is more than sufficient. The number of times you spray is important. Three represents a holy trinity.

After you've anointed, get the fire started: light your candle(s) and/or incense.

Make Your Offerings

If you're using smoke, run the items you're offering over and through the smoke to cleanse them and then 'present' them to your ancestors. This can be done by holding the item and then lifting it as if you were giving a gift to someone much taller than you.

Do this activity with your whole being. Imagine your benevolent ancestors coming around and graciously accepting what you offer.

Dial In

Read Psalms 23. If you don't have a bible, look the prayer up online. There are also many bible apps available for free and with no ads.

Call on your ancestors. Here's an example of what you might want to say. Feel free to edit or change according to your needs: I now call on the benevolent and honored spirits of my lineage, every man and woman who sired and birthed the men and women who now live through me.

I invite you into my home and into my life. This altar is where we will meet, and where I will offer my deep gratitude for the sacrifices you've made and the work you continue to do on my behalf.

I offer you [name the items you've offered in the form of food, scents, items, etc.] with honor, love, and thanks. I hope they are pleasing to you.

You don't have to make the call super formal. I would actually recommend telling your ancestors that you're just starting on this journey, that this is the first time you are working with them (though there's a good chance they know already). You can also ask for guidance on your relationship with them. Be open to even the smallest ways that they speak to you.

Once you say that your altar is the place where you will meet and offer gratitude, you have to actually use your altar to meet your ancestors and offer gratitude when you get there. This ritual is about making a commitment to a relationship. What you say in this meeting is important, so take note.

Get Comfortable

Spend some time in silence, just listening. You may receive guidance on things you're dealing with right now. Or you may just feel feelings, like love, peace, or just a general good You Are Blessed feeling. Sit as long as you like. You will intuitively feel when your time at the altar is complete.

Close

I keep closings very simple at my altar. I simply clasp my hands, close my eyes, and feel gratitude throughout my body. This is my everyday practice, and since you're doing a first-time ritual at your altar, you may want to do something more formal.

In your practice, you'll come across countless more altar and ritual ideas, some you'll work, and others you'll let go by.

Creating an Altar in Your Mind

This is an option to consider if you don't have space for an altar or aren't really interested in creating a physical space in your home, as described.

To Spirit, everything is energy. Our physical world helps us humans with that, but for spirit, these physical things don't mean much. This is why intent is so important. You can (and do) create a whole world in your mind and without intention, you can create a lot without being aware.

Creating an altar in your mind uses visualization, an important skill that some people find easier than others.

You can create a whole castle in your mind that is an altar, then speak to your ancestors and the spirits you are calling to let them know that space is for them. If you are unable to purchase or find the items for your altar, you can just imagine them. Or better yet, create them in your mind and place them in your mind altar.

The Choose Your Adventure Altar

Whereas there are specific rules for ancestors, you can create an altar for whatever you want to draw into your life. Remember how everything has a spirit? Creating an altar is basically honoring these spirits.

You can create an altar for style, peace, and serenity, beauty, a season, a career you want, good health, education, a sport, a craft, for a loving family, cooking, the elements, even a place, maybe somewhere you want to live, like a cottage or a farm.

Holidays in Hoodoo

Days of feast and charged power

JANUARY 6-8th: Feast Days of Jasper, Balthazar & Melchior (For obtaining gifts & prosperity). 17th: Ogun (For work, opportunities, protection from accidents and firearms).

FEBRUARY 2nd: Oyá, Mistress of the Cemetery (For a change, readying for battle, protection from weather).

MARCH 19th: Osanyin (Deciduous vegetation, for healing and nourishment from Nature). 25th: Oshun - Our Lady of Charity. For love, abundance, charity, passion, creativity (See also September).

APRIL 22nd: Earth Day - All Loa and Orisha (For renewing one's vows to make one's life sacred and in harmony with the whole Creation)

MAY 15th: Ochosi - The Divine Hunter -(For justice, court cases, re-establishing balance and universal harmony)

JUNE 21-23rd: Summer Solstice - Legba - St John's Eve - John the Conqueror. To celebrate the summer, the warmth, fire and nourishment from the Sun. (For opportunities, good luck and to re-align with cosmic forces)

AUGUST 2nd: Black Madonna - Virgin of the Angels. For solace, protection, fertility, to give up one's sorrows and for protection of mothers and children.)

SEPTEMBER 7th: Yemayá (For appeasement of sorrows, abundance, love and fertility, protection of the home). 8th: Oshun -Our Lady of Charity (For love, abundance, charity, passion, creativity, the Arts. (See also March) 24th: Obatalá - Our Lady of Mercy (For universal peace and harmony).

OCTOBER 4th: Orunmila (For divination, psychic powers, prophetic knowledge) 24th: Erinle (For healing all) 31st: Halloween (to make hallowed before the rites of the Ancestors - to dispel evil forces through disguise and trickery)

NOVEMBER 1st: Day of the Dead - Baron Samedi - Manman Brigitte - Ghede (Rites to the Ancestors according to your own familial or ethnic tradition) 3rd: St Martin de Porres (For healing and for those who have made healing professions their chosen path)

DECEMBER 4th: Changó (For vitality, health, courage, victory in battles, to repel enemies and negative works and evil spells)

12th: Our Lady of Guadalupe (For miracles, for abundance, solace in times of trials and troubles, healing and for strengthening one's faith) 17th: Babalú-Ayé (For healing, particularly skin ailments, for abundance) 21-25th: Winter Solstice - Christmas - Ellegua - El Nino de Atocha – Infant Jesus of Prague. (To celebrate the coming return of the sun, to prepare for the winter months and their unseen transformation, which will lead to new birth in springtime, to re-align with the cosmic forces. Birth of Jesus celebration 31st: Yemayá - La Madre de Agua. (For the protection of mothers and children, for fertility and abundance, to usher a new year of compassion and well-being and wealth in all things).

CHAPTER 10: MOJO BAGS GRIS-GRIS TALISMAN BOTTLE TRESES JACK BALL

Hoodoo Inks

Any spells or rituals that require special ink to write name sheets and the like require the use of this ink. Among the earliest forms include Egyptian ink, different natural metal colors, the husk or outer covering of beans or seeds, and sea critters such as the cuttlefish (known as sepia). Indian ink is dark pink with an Asian heritage. Many of the old masters utilized iron gall ink to sketch. Using abundant berries, plants, and minerals, early cultures generated a variety of pink hues.

Scribes in medieval Europe (about AD 800–1550) used sheepskin parchment to write. In one 12th-century ink recipe, hawthorn branches were harvested and dried in the spring. After pounding the bark off the branches, it was steeped in water for eight days.

The water was brought to a boil and allowed to thicken and darken. The wine was added when the mixture was boiling. The ink was placed into special bags and allowed to dry in the sunlight. After drying, the mixture was heated and combined with wine and iron salt to make the final ink. In China, around 5000 years ago, ink for blackening the raised surfaces of stone images and writings was invented. This early ink was composed of soot from pine smoke, lamp oil, gelatin derived from animal skins, and musk.

Rather than creating your inks or using the prescribed ink, you can dedicate an ordinary pen in the proper color for ritual usage. Based on the Key of Solomon the King, this ritual will prepare your pen for use in rituals.

Recite the following while holding your pen up in front of you: ADRAI, HAHLII, TAMAH, TILONAS, ATHAMAS, ZIANOR, ADONAI, cleanse my pen of all deception and mistake, so I may write everything that I wish with virtue and efficacy. Indeed, Amen.

Now, smudge the area with fragrant incense such as sandalwood, sprinkle it with holy water, and set it away in a silken robe of any color other than black or grey.

Some modern formulas for three popular links have been included below for anyone so motivated.

The Ink of the Bat

- High-quality ink

- Cinnamon absolute essential oil

- Essential myrrh oil

Combine all ingredients and use them as ink for writing spells.

The Ink of the Dove

- High-quality ink

- Rose essential oil

Combine ingredients to create love spells and talismans.

The Ink of the Dragon

Dragon's blood is a term that refers to the vibrant red gum resin produced by the Dragon palm tree. In ancient times, the red resin was utilized as varnish, medicine, incense, and color. It was utilized in medieval alchemy and ritual magic. Some continue to use Magickal Inks for the objectives mentioned above. It is used in Hoodoo for money-drawing or love-drawing and as a fragrance to cleanse an area of negative beings or influences. Additionally, it is added with red ink to develop "Dragon's Blood Ink," which is used for engraving mystical seals and talismans. To make your own Dragon's Blood Ink, you will need the following ingredients: • High-quality ink • Resin from Dragon tree Combine to create talismans of good fortune or protection.

Hoodoo Powders

Gris (pronounced as gree-gree) is a phrase used in New Orleans to refer to a form of grey magic and mojo used by many hoodoos. Grey magic, often known as neutral magic, is a type of magic that is not practiced purely for positive causes but is not fully hostile either. It is thought to be between black and white magic. The term "mojo" is originally related to an African-inspired amulet or magical charm. Though the history is obscure, it may be connected in form and concept to "moco'o," a West African term for "medicine man." There is a gris-gris for everything. Gris-gris is whatever mixture you make for any given scenario. Frequently, gris-gris is used in foot track works. Gris may be made with various ingredients, including powdered minerals, herbs, cemetery dust, and roots.

Powders are frequently utilized in hoodoo spell work. They are used in spells to create charms, adorn letters, job applications, and business cards, combine with other powders, and work with foot track magick. Sulfur, cemetery soil, salt, and pepper are the most often used constituents in these powders.

Here are a few recipes to get you started. You will learn to use these powders in spells and crossroads as you proceed to read the book. You just have to put the powders in a bag and place them at the location you want to execute your spells.

Aunt Sally's Dream Powder

Make sure that some of this results in prophetic dreams. Before retiring to bed, sprinkle on your linens.

- Licorice

- Cardamom

- Cinnamon

- Coriander

Grind herbs and add them into rice flour or corn starch base.

Powder of Blessings

- Lavandin

- Indian sandalwood

- Rosemary

- Sand that is magnetic

Grind herbs and combine with magnetic sand in rice flour or corn starch base.

Powder for Control

- Corn starch

- Sodium chloride

- Epsom salts

Drawing Powder

- Magnetic sand

- Corn gluten meal

- Sucrose (confectioner's sugar)

Add to rice flour or corn starch base.

Goofer Dust

Goofer Dust is an extremely ancient African-American hoodoo mixture designed to inflict great hardship, damage, or even death to an adversary. Several recipes are not likely to reflect the conjuror's goal. If the necessary substances are added to goofer dust, it can also be employed for its protective characteristics.

Goofer dust in its purest form comprises the following:

- Mausoleum soil

- Snakeskin

- Sesame seed

- Magnetic sand

- Sulfur granules

To this basic mixture, other ingredients such as pulverized insects, powdered bones, or black pepper would be added to increase its effects.

Graveyard dust

Graveyard soil was collected from nine different graveyards, including one from a child's grave for good deeds and one or more from a criminal's tomb for evil deeds.

Hot Foot Powder

- Chili powder

- Black pepper

- Red pepper

- Sulfur

Mix a rice flour or corn starch base.

Jinx Removing Powder

- Wintergreen

- Mint

- Chamomile

Grind herbs and add them into rice flour or corn starch base.

Money Drawing Powder

- Patchouli

- Cedar

- Ginger

- Galangal

Grind herbs and add them into rice flour or corn starch base.

Gris Bags

Gris bags are usually carried in dolls or bags and are essentially used to transport charms or spells. Marie Laveau was most known for her powerful gris-gris charms, which comprised a magical sign or vévé written on parchment paper using Dragon's blood ink and sewed into fabric or leather bags. Her consumers shelled out hundreds of dollars for these charms and swore by their efficacy.

A gris-gris bag is traditionally a two-inch by three-inch drawstring bag crafted of red flannel, leather into which some things are written and placed on something.

For Example,

- Special Herbs

- Chamois

- Stones

- Personal Effects

- Coins

- Roots

- Bones

- Lucky Metal Charms

- Carved Stones

- Crystals

- Good Luck Tokens

- European Sigils and Seals

These things are written and placed on parchment paper.

Additionally, colors can also be employed following their magickal meanings, as mentioned in the earlier chapters. Your gris-gris bag should include an odd amount of items; no fewer than three and no more than thirteen. As the items are put into the bag, they are blessed, and the entire bag is anointed with anointing oil. It is then smeared with incense or inhaled to trigger the magic.

This is similar to a talisman, except that it is concealed from public view. It is always cooked next to an altar in a ritualistic fashion. Bear in mind the following five considerations while "repairing" a gris-gris bag:

The significance of color symbolism. Select a hue that is appropriate for your situation.

- It must include an odd quantity of pieces, more than three but not exceeding thirteen.

- It should be stocked with purpose-specific items.

- It must be prepared in some liquid.

- It is also smeared or smoked in incense, candles, or when breathed.

To utilize a gris-gris bag, grasp it and direct your attention to a need or desire. Imagine yourself achieving your objective by developing a vivid mental image of yourself achieving what you desire. As regularly as possible, perform this exercise. Keep it in a prominent location to serve as a reminder of your desire or need. Men often wear them on their right side, while women often wear them on their left sides.

Talismans

A talisman is a tiny amulet or another artifact, frequently imprinted with mystical symbols, to ward off bad spirits or the supernatural. Drawings are employed as talismans or amulets and placed in mojo bags in Afro-Caribbean syncretic faiths such as Hoodoo, Voodoo, Umbanda, Quimbanda, and Santera. Other signs, such as magic squares, heavenly signatures, Solomon's seals, and kabbalistic signs, have been used for benign and malignant purposes. Each of these is used in Hoodoo.

Horseshoes are regarded as a good luck charm in a wide variety of cultures. A widespread belief is that if a horseshoe is placed on a door with its two ends pointing upward, it will bring good fortune. However, if both ends point downward, misfortune will strike. However, traditions diverge on this issue. In some cultures, the horseshoe is hung pointed down (so that the luck flows over you); in others, it is hung pointed up (so that the luck does not fall out); and in still others, it is irrelevant as long as the horseshoe has been used (not new), was discovered (not purchased), and is touchable. In every tradition, fortune is housed within the shoe and may be released through the ends.

The difference in effect between an amulet and a talisman is minor. Some practitioners of magick believe that amulets should be charged while the moon is declining, and talismans should be charged when the moon is waxing.

Talismans are relatively common in diverse cultures throughout the world. They are used for protection and purification, offerings to deities, as charms or amulets protecting against evil influences, as good luck objects or talismans of power. A person with a knowledge of these practices can create such a talisman using traditional forms and techniques or create them using materials available to him/her. The practice of creating these charms is known in some cultures as Hoodoo, a term also used in Vodou hand-dancing for the creation of protective circles who practice this art.

Consecration of a Talisman

Consecrate your amulets and talismans and amulets. To accomplish this, take these steps: As a sacrifice to the Divine, light some incense (or whatever you feel is your greater power), three white candles, arranged in a triangular shape on your altar, should be lit.

Sprinkle salt on the amulet/talisman.

"I sanctify you with the Earth element so that you will emanate a protective aura around the person who holds you."

Through the incense, pass the amulet/talisman.

"I sanctify you with the element of Air, in the hope that you will emanate a protective aura around whoever holds you."

Through the candle flame, pass the amulet/talisman.

"I sanctify you with the element of Fire, in the hope that you would emanate a protective aura around whoever holds you."

Water the amulet/talisman.

"I sanctify you with the element of Water, in the hope that you will emanate a protective aura around whoever holds you."

Reintroduce the amulet/talisman to your altar. Both hands should be placed over the amulet/talisman.

Visualize a stream of white light streaming into the amulet/talisman from above.

"I entrust this amulet/talisman with the duty of (insert its function) since I [your name] am a Divine servant. Thus be it!"

Put out your candles (always pinch out the flame, never blow).

Your Talisman or Amulet is now complete and ready to be worn.

Uses of Talismans

In your mojo bags, country sacks, and gris-gris bags, incorporate the following talismans. Copies of the ones you require and place them in your gris-gris bags to amp up their magickal properties. To draw the finest results, trace the talisman onto parchment paper using Dragon's blood ink. Alternatively, you can print the page, cut out the appropriate talisman, and fold it either toward you or away from you to draw the talisman's qualities.

Exu Loa:

The ritual emblem for Exu, the god of crossroads. Utilize to remove impediments and create opportunities.

Square Satori:

The Sator Square is a word square containing a Latin palindrome consisting of the phrases SATOR AREPO TENET OPERA ROTAS arranged in a square so that they can be read in ascendiung, descending and sideways orders. Use to remove jinxes and hexes, protect against evil influences, and combat tiredness when traveling.

The Pentagram:

A pentagram is a five-pointed star formed by five straight strokes. As an amulet, it can be used to attract money, love, and other blessings and protect against envy, misfortune, and other embarrassments.

Love:

This amulet design is taken from the Black Pullet grimoire. The Black Pullet is a grimoire that purports to instruct readers in the "science of magical talismans and rings," including necromancy and Kabbalah.

It is said that if you embroider it on black satin and say "Nades,

Suradis, Maniner," a djinn will arrive; if you tell the djinn "Sader, Prostas, Solaster," the djinn will bring you true love. When you have had enough of her, say, "Mammes, Laher."

Clover with Four Leaves:

The clover, which originated with the medieval Celts, signifies good luck if it has four leaves.

Power:

Utilize when you need to end a relationship or scenario. It is possible to use this against a person, but it is not suggested.

Sexual Potency:

Loa Erzulie Freda is a talisman for sexual potency.

To Invoke Celestial Forces:

Utilize this talisman to summon infernal and celestial forces. Make a talisman ring with the bottom words written inside the ring's band. Put the talisman on your finger, place it over your heart, and then say these words: Siras, Etar, Besanar, and you will feel the results.

For Wealth and Prosperity:

This talisman will assist you in discovering all available treasures and ensuring your possession of them. Make a ring for the talisman, ensuring that the bottom characters are inscribed on the inside of the ring. Put the ring on your right-hand second finger, encircle the talisman with your left thumb and little finger, and say, Onaim, Perantes, Rasonastos. Seven bronze-colored spirits will approach, each carrying a big hide bag brimming with riches that will be emptied at your feet.

Seal of the Archangels' Choir of Ministering Archangels:

This seal's great secret and unique function is that it will rise to the surface on its own accord during a full moon if it is placed in the dirt near treasures.

Mojo Bags

A mojo bag is a very popular working in hoodoo. It is also one of the first things you want to create as you start your practice.

The hoodoo definition of mojo is spirit.

We talked about containment in a previous section. This is a concept specific to the Yoruba tradition out of western Africa.

A mojo bag is about concentrating the energy of spirit in work towards whatever your intent.

You generally can't go wrong when creating one of these for your personal use. You can find many, many spells for mojo bags online or in hoodoo books. It makes a great first spell for beginners because you are encouraged to get creative.

One practitioner I know used a name necklace that broke in such a way that their name was split almost in half. She wasn't interested in getting the piece fixed, but she also didn't care to throw it away because it meant something to her. The broken necklace made a perfect addition to her self-love mojo bag. Her intent in creating the bag was to heal a broken spirit.

Generally, the purpose of these bags is to draw love, money, success, or protection to you. You can use it while you're working to create a larger change in your life.

Let's say, for example, that you want to draw in real romantic love. Not just a new boyfriend or girlfriend (or boyfriends or girlfriends), but a true shift in your outlook on love.

You know, however, that this will require a change in your mindset and you're not sure about what this will look or feel like.

With a mojo bag, you can get help making this deeper shift so that when your love spell works, you don't block the love you deserve.

The rules for a mojo bag are simple:

No one but you is to touch, see, or use your mojo bag for any reason. We're all used to keeping things in secret; that applies here as well.

You can either keep it on you all the time or every day over a period, like a week or lunar cycle, depending on what you're using it for.

Making a Mojo Bag

It might seem excessive to buy a whole yard of flannel online just to create a relatively small item. Another option may be searching through your closet to see if you have any flannel that will work or checking with anyone who may want to donate some fabric to you.

However, most flannel is available cheaply priced, and if you enjoy making a mojo bag with enough fabric, you can make bags for your friends and family.

You want to create a mojo bag with intention, in the same way that you would create your altar.

You can also imagine that the items that go inside can include things you would put on an altar; curios (small items like figurines and symbols), herbs, oils (usually in small glass jars or containers), crystals and energy stones, dried plants, petitions to spirit, hair or fingernails, coins and dollar bills, jewelry, and, of course, roots.

There are two different ways you can make one of these bags for yourself, depending on how comfortable you are with a needle and thread. For the mojo bags below, you will need your flannel and string, again, in a color that *speaks* to you and your working. However, the simple and effective choice in many cases may be to go with your favorites.

Before creating your mojo bag, you'll want to do a good cleanse and pray over *everything* you'll be using to create and make your bag.

One thing I have not included in the ingredient lists below is *you*. In each mojo bag you create for yourself, you must include inside something that has your DNA, your energetic signature. This can be as simple as the breath.

After all of the ingredients, adding your breath can be saying your intention at the mouth of the bag or over the ingredients inside. You want your breath to come into contact with the ingredients you've put inside.

Other than your breath, you can include hair, toenails, fingernails, spit, blood, anything that comes from your body. Most practitioners would recommend adding some substance of yours, such as your toenails and your breath.

You want to keep your mojo bag as close as possible to your body for at least a week.

The advantage of the sewing option is the ability to create a satchel that can hold more than the non-sewing option.

The Sewing Option

Cut a piece of flannel cloth, 4 inches wide by 12 inches long.

Fold the flannel in half on the "wrong" side so the bag is 4 inches wide by 6 inches long.

Sew inside about a quarter inch along the long edges, leaving the top open.

Flip inside out, and now you have a little bag.

Pray over and bless each item before putting it inside. As you fill your bag, you will start to feel the energy building.

Tie a string around the closure or create a simple drawstring.

The Non-Sewing Option

This type of mojo bag is commonly called a 'flaming comet' because once tied closed, it looks like a comet.

You'll want to cut your flannel in the shape of a square; 5 in x 5 in is sufficient. The idea is to put all of your materials in the middle and then gather the ends and secure the string around, so everything is contained tightly inside.

Ingredient Lists

Each recipe has a few color options for your flannel. You'll also find most recipes include: a small symbolic object, a natural element (such as a root or dried herb), one or two crystals.

Do not include anything in your mojo bag that you don't connect with, or that doesn't mean anything to you.

Another name for a mojo bag is a 'hand'. An apt name, since to make these bags, you use your hands. If your energy is off in any way, that is going to transfer through your body, through your hands, and go into the bag you're creating.

Before you begin praying and cleansing, get as calm as possible. If you can't get calm, choose another date or time to create the bag. Create a feeling of excitement. As you create your bag, keep in mind that you're getting everything you want, and the specific circumstances that led you to create this mojo bag! Think and agree with yourself that every item you're using to create your bag will *work for you.*

A few elements listed below are universal, meaning you can use them for any of the bags listed. Instead of going for a generic green, for example, choose a shade that aligns with your intent. For an inner peace or inner healing mojo bag you might go with sage green, while for the money, you could use an emerald green.

In addition, often you'll find crystals that are molded into different shapes, for example, a rose quartz in the shape of a heart or a jade stone in the shape of a frog. These objects can do double or triple duty in your mojo bag if used with intention.

I should note that while white is a universal shade for magic, a mojo bag is created to be carried with you all the time, which would mean it may show dirt easily. Consider using white for the items you place inside of your bag. Otherwise, be prepared to clean your bag constantly.

<u>Colors to Choose for Your Mojo Bag</u>

- **Gold:** This works with the Sun and encourages wealth and success combined with projectivity. The god yang is linked with gold, and he provides a loud, in-your-face type of energy.

- **Silver:** Working with the moon, the goddess yin is linked with this color and promotes meditative processes and peace.

- **Red:** Connected to the planet Mars, passion and courage are associated with this hue. The deeper the red, the more energetic the mojo.

- **Orange:** Associated with the planet Mercury, orange is the color of success. It helps give the ingredients of the bag the power of vitality and speed.

- **Yellow:** Governed by the Sun, yellow is the color of joy and creativity. Bring an aura of allure to your spells when you store your tools in this bag.

- **Green:** working with the planet Venus your bag will be imbued with the power of good fortune and wealth.

- **Blue:** Associated with the planet Jupiter use blue material to bring wisdom and rhetoric to your spells. This is the color of intelligence and represents the deep connection you have mentally with the spirits.

- **Violet:** This striking color is all about healing and aiding karmic connections. Tools kept in this bag will be powerful when connecting to the spiritual world or using divination connections.

- **Rose Pink:** This is the color of love and friendship. Use it to enhance your romantic and creative skills and increase personal beauty.

- **White:** The classic color of divination and spirituality. This bag will help you connect to angels and improve your psychological health.

- **Grey:** Objects stored in grey bags will become mysterious and will be powerful when creating illusions. They will be powerful in spells involving invisibility and secretive moves.

- **Black:** Banishing spells and protection rituals will work better with a black mojo bag. The planet Saturn is associated with this color and provides a level of discipline.

Tips to Help You Name Your Bag

- Listen to your heart. Once you have made your bag, you will begin to hear certain names or see a sign that indicates what to call your bag. You may dream of meeting a woman called Mary and then see the name in the press a couple of times. This will help you decide what to call your bag.

- For a more off-the-wall name, you need to pick a person who symbolizes the endeavor you want your bag to represent. For instance, if you want to attract wealth, call your bag Elon or Bezos after the tech giants. Love mojo bags should be called Romeo or Cupid to signify their connection to romance. The base idea is your bag will take on the characteristics of the person after whom it is named.

- Look to your faith. If you are of a certain faith, then biblical names will be suitable. Samson is a great name for strength, while Adam means living. Research your choices with a baby name book to discover what different names mean.

- Let the spirits guide you. Take a random book from your bookshelf and let it fall open. There will be a name there that shouts to you and tells you what to call your bag.

Once your bag is loaded, blessed, and named, it's time to make it part of your being. For the first week, your need to keep it close to your skin. Pin it inside your clothes or wear it around your neck so it can imbue your spirit and become part of your psyche. At night pin it to the base of your pillow or keep it on your nightstand. Feed it with magic oil regularly during that first week and keep it dry and clean.

How Long Does the Mojo Bag Work?

1) Your bag is for your eyes only. If someone else sees or touches your bag, it can "kill your hand" and render the mojo inactive.

2) Hard items should be taken out and cleaned, while soft items like herbs and petals need to be replaced when needed.

3) Feed the bag every week on the same day as it was made by using oil to regenerate its power. Use incense smoke and prayer to feed the bag whenever you need to call upon it.

4) Keep your bag dry. If it gets wet, attempt to revive its power with the Rose of Jericho plant, aka the resurrection plant.

5) There is no reason to replace your bag after a year if it's still working for you. Time and strength can differ, and different bags work better than others. Only you will know when to make a new bag and dispose of your old one.

6) When you decide to replace your bag, treat it with respect and bury it with care. This manifestation tool has been good to you, and you need to acknowledge that.

Storing Your Mojo Bags

After the first week, store your bag carefully so it will work correctly. Choose a hardwood box that is decorative and well-sealed. Place your bag inside and choose a candle to sit on the lid. Light the candle and burn it until the wax reaches the bottom of the box. This will form a sacred seal that will protect your bag until you need it.

Your mojo bag can be customized to suit any need. If you are looking for a new job, you can use a green bag filled with gravel root and magnetizing salt to draw well-paid employment into your life. If you are unfortunate enough to be falsely accused of a crime, then a blend of sage, galangal (aka court case root), and other herbs will help you get your case across in court. Use your mojo bag to confuse the opposition and get the judge or jury to rule in your favor.

If you prefer to buy commercial mojo bags, know the terms "double strength" or "triple strength." Ideally, this will mean the bag contains curios that are less readily available, like a human bone or a snake rib, but sometimes it just means there are more than the normal amount of items inside. Commercial bags do work, but you empower them with your essence and spirit when you make them yourself. Hoodoo is a powerful way to protect yourself, and commercial bags are less personal but can still be effective.

CHAPTER 11: CEMETERIES

If it is easy to understand the development environment and hoodoo history, it is less easy to understand the practice environment. The first one we will examine is familiar to everyone, although it arouses different reactions; it is the cemetery.

The hoodoo rituals and spells that involve visits to the cemetery are many and to avoid ending up in topics that could be judged morbid, we will only say the extreme limits that can be reached in the practice of the root doctor. The minimum is to pray at the cemetery or use cemetery earth (usually a few grams) taken from particular graves' outer surfaces to make amulets and powders. The maximum is to light votive candles on a tomb or bury a small fetish on the side. Another traditional practice is to use human bones or teeth in amulets. Usually, they are small fragments or bones of phalanges that, however, you never go and never go to dig up at the cemetery since human bones, in Anglo-Saxon countries, can be safely purchased from stores specializing in anatomical models, which can provide the parts individually or deliver entire skeletons, mounted with special attachments to scholars, artists or anatomy enthusiasts.

It is interesting to reflect that one often cares about the bones of poor animals and no one blinks an eye when anonymous skeletons of strangers who have died in China or India are sold piece by piece. Homo homini lupus. However, at most in the past, it could happen to use ashes of their own extinct or to buy from some complacent cemetery keeper a small bone fragment today the practice is much less widespread. In Italy, however, all this is prohibited by the current laws, and therefore we will not describe any amulet that uses such objects.

Concerning other cemetery practices, we will describe later only the simplest, which is also basic in hoodoo: to "buy land" at the cemetery; land that, today, can also be bought in specialized stores.

Obviously, the most sensitive mentalities are shocked or shaken by this familiarity with death and the dead. The psychology of the root doctor, however, is very different from that of the normal well-thinking. The conjure man does not see the cemetery as a place of ancestral fears and "bad thoughts," for him it is not a place of death, but a place of life and especially of sacred power. It is the place for a different form of life, with which one can communicate, which one can celebrate, which is often "familiar" in the true sense of the word. The root doctor thinks of the dead as alive and well and able to autonomously dispose of what they have to give. It may seem absurd for the mentality accustomed to the sacred reverential fear of earthly remains, but the Tibetan Buddhist monk who offers the buddha drinks in cups made from human skulls, or blows during ceremonies in flutes made with shins of old llamas does not do anything different from the conjure man; he does much more, only that generally, for his peaceful demeanor, is much more sympathetic to public opinion.

CHAPTER 12: HOODOO SIGILS

LOA Mystery

In Hoodoo, many spirits are worshiped that are referred to as Loa (mystery), and these spirits are invoked and nourished during voodoo or woodoo rituals, and there is a belief in the presence of supernatural forces in plants, objects, and people. On various occasions, voodoo rituals celebrate special events such as births, deaths, and weddings or to obtain help from the Loa spirits and keep him "happy" and nourish him through the rituals. According to this religion, each person would have two spirits: a great guardian spirit and a minor spirit, a small guardian spirit, and it would be possible for the small guardian spirit to leave the body during sleep or during certain types of rituals and could be captured by other entities that make up the Loa.

Some deities that make up the Loa are called **Afra, Asojano, Afreqete, Hevioso**.

The preachers of voodoo rituals, if they are men, are called hungan, if they are women, are called mambo. Voodoo rituals last an entire night and are so organized:

Sacious chants accompanied by drum rolls for the duration of the ritual, the drums are three, of increasing size, the smallest is called bula, the middle is called segond, and the largest is called manman.

Frenzied dances called Ararà accompanied by physical beatings to the dancers.

Sacrificial animals such as chickens, goats, chickens, or dogs are slaughtered during the ritual, the blood of the sacrificial animals is sometimes drunk, and the blood poured into the ground instead serves to feed the Loa as the spirits that have the same function, to feed the Loa.

Use of herbal extracts, spices, and drugs

Each Loa has a particular type of sound made with the drum and a specific sacrificial animal and dance. During a ritual, a dancer can fall into a trance with convulsions and tremors, finding himself possessed by Loa's spirit that communicates with the whole village through the body of the dancer. The trance of these people sometimes lasts for hours but can last for days.

The Meaning of Loa

Often the Voodoo religion is considered polytheistic, but that's not the case... The Loa are the deities through which the "God of the Gods" of Voodoo is manifested. The unique and powerful God is seen in Voodoo, far away from the man. The distance of the Bon Dieu is because, in its immensity, it cannot be grasped by human reason in its totality, as it is infinite. But He does not want to be far from man, so He is divided into a series of divinities that are part of Him and are closer in fact to man. These divinities are comprehensible to the human intellect as laws, behaviors, manifestations that in Haitian Voodoo take the name of Loa and that in Africa were simply called Vodun.

Loa has a value, a number, and is understandable. We can practically compare them to the angels of the Jewish tradition.

Although in the Poem there are 401, in reality, the Loa are many more, almost infinite, since new ones could be born every day. They have intelligence, and they are immortal, yet they are subject to a time and, once their mission is over, they can be absorbed by Bon Dieu and return, perhaps in a different form and in other eras.

Although the myth refers to Him as the Great Old Man, in reality, He is androgynous, Father and Mother at the same time.

God, the Father is called Lihsah Bha God and contains the powers of the Sun, the first from which all the male figures in the pantheon derive.

Mother God is called Mawu and contains the powers of the moon, the first from which all the female figures of the pantheon derive.

Mawu and Lihsah are not Loa, but in them, all Loa vibrate. The Loa derive from them when they descend in Damballah and Aida's guise, beginning the history of man and the world.

Loa are divided into families (fanmi) and nations (nanchòn). A family groups the various manifestations of the Loa itself plus any Loa that vibrate together with this Loa. The nations indicate the origin and the mode of worship of a particular Loa.

Loa Manifestations

The manifestations of the Loa are true crossings of energetic vibrations. These in Voodoo are called points. The point indicates a force, a power, energy coming from a spiritual source.

A point of Danbhallah Pethro, which defines itself as Bord de la Mer, will indicate a manifestation of Danbhallah Pethro which is honored on the bramble of the sea, which crosses its energy with that of Agwé (male Loa of the sea) and which in its offerings will require elements typical of Danbhallah Pethro and Agwé.

The point theory is fundamental. It is not easy to understand which Loa holds a person's head; only possession can reveal the arcane. In Voodoo, the first one who rides an individual's head will necessarily be his Met Tet. But this first Loa is not always defined. In this case, the theory of points will be fundamental to allow us to recognize the quality or mode of the Loa, specifying its essence and making it possible to interpret its esoteric and religious meaning.

Although magic practice tends to give each Loa a specific task, in reality each Loa can act on several fronts, so a person who is a child of a specific Loa will be able to turn to this for each problem, even if this does not prevent him/her from winking at other Loa and turning to them.

As for African traditions, it is always necessary to ask a Loa, through cards, through dreams or through a child's possession, if the Loa is willing to help and in what terms.

In New Orleans, in addition to these systems, the 4 shells (the Yoruba oracle of Oborí) or the divination practice of dice are used. Some use candles to scan the flame for answers; others use a magic mirror.

Danbhallah Family

The most important mystery of the Voodoo tradition is the androgynous snake Danbhallah Wedo - Aida Wedo.

Da(n) = snake

Dan Gbè = Sacred Serpent, whose esoteric meaning is:

Dan = Snake

Gbe/a = of life, which dispenses life

The snake in the Voodoo tradition is a symbol of knowledge and understanding; it is God who allows man to be understood and who does great things for him. The snake Dan represents the mystery of the Incarnation.

According to the Poem, all Loa are children of Danbhallah and his comoagna Aida. Their children are generally calm and reserved individuals and have great willpower; they do not allow themselves to be influenced. They have a great sense of adaptation. They are led to reflection and knowledge. Usually, they are individuals of a good economic situation.

Danbhallah is depicted as a snake plowing the sky following the solar course, accompanied by the rainbow, his wife, Aida. It is a celestial Loa but is also associated with the element water and is usually invoked to bring peace, wealth and rain. In her honor, leaf baths are prepared to eliminate evil or propitiate fate.

Danbhallah We Do

The suffix We Do comes from the etymology of the royal family of the kingdom of Oidah in West Africa. The Loa with this suffix belongs to the solar rite Rada and are distinguished by their benevolence and magnanimity. The sun in Voodoo is the star and the living and visible symbol of the Ville aux Champs, from which all Loa come and reside.

Danbhallah We Do embodies good, it is the old father of the man. He is the patron saint and lord of the waters of heaven. He is made a creature with St. Patrick. During the trance, his spiritual children crawl like snakes and hiss like snakes. One of his famous daughters was Marie Laveau. In the myth, he is the one who causes earthquakes. He is invoked for wealth, good fortune, and success.

Festivity: 17th March

Day of the week: Thursday or Sunday

Beverage: milk, barley syrup

Color: white, white and green

Metal: silver

Number: 7 and 2

Flowers: White flowers, iris

Fruit: Coconut, grape, pineapple

Perfume: magnolia, linden

Plate: ceramic

Food offers: white-shelled eggs resting on a small mountain of flour, condensed milk, snake-shaped gummy candies, white and yellow corn flour, honey, rice, rice flour, chickpeas, coconut, sweet potatoes, almonds, soya, meringues, white and juicy fruit

Homage: silver coins, white candles, candles of 7 colors, ceramic basin with water

Place of power: springs, riverbanks

Planet: sun

Ritual necklace: made of white glass beads

Aida, We Do

She is the wife of Danbhallah We Do, from their union would be born Legbha.

She is the lady of the rainbow and wealth; she is represented as the Virgin of Hautegrace. She is Queen of Heaven, Earth, and all Angels.

She protects trade and is conducive to fertility and pregnancy.

Her spiritual daughters are sparkling, impulsive, love to chat and joke, love children and have a strong sense of justice. They are often invoked in rites of love and union and when they wish to change their lifestyle.

Festivities: 21st January

Day of the week: Tuesday, Saturday

Beverage: sparkling wine, milk

Color: white and blue

Metal: gold

Number: 7, 6

Flower: Amapola, white iris

Fruit: coconut

Perfume: amber

Plate: ceramic

Food offers: white shell eggs on which rainbow colors are traced with chalk, white or yellow corn flour, milk cakes, honey, rice, rice flour, chickpeas, coconut, sweet potatoes, duck, pigeon

Homage: golden coins, sweet scents, white and blue candles, candles of 7 colors, snake-shaped jewelry colored with the seven colors of the iris

Place of power: springs, riverbanks

Ritual necklace: formed by beads of the 7 colors of the iris or soft blue balls

Planet: moon

Danbhallah Nagò/Ocumare

In this Loa, we recognize the well-known Orixà Oxumarè from the Yoruba pantheon. Protector of wealth and change, he embodies the mystery of transmutation and continuous movement. His female counterpart is Ewà.

Festivity: 24th August

Day of the week: Tuesday

Beverage: milk

Color: the 7 colors of the iris

Metal: silver

Number: 7

Flower: evergreen

Fruit: coconut

Perfume: Mandarin

Plate: ceramic

Food offers: eggs, white corn, honey, rice, rice, chickpeas, and sweet potatoes

Homage: silver coins

Place of power: under the trees

Ritual necklace: made of white powder shells

Planet: uran

Danbhallah Pethro/Danbhallah Le Flambeau

This manifestation, cultured in the fire ritualistic Pethro, embodies God's wrath, anger in the face of the wicked and those who go against his laws. He is depicted as a snake of fire and always accompanied by his wife, Erzulie Jé Rouge. He is the head of the phalanx of all Loa Pethro and Congo Savane. He protects crops and those who work the land. He is vindictive and violent. The Loa, even though it is Pethro, is cultured according to the Congo rite. Some people worship it with Moses. According to the myth, the father of Ti Jean Pethro is the spirit of Jean Philippe Pedro, the Dominican who founded the Pethro cult in Haiti.

He is invoked to punish those who commit serious injustices. Its strength is not maliciously destructive; it can be used in a strong opposition or when you find powerful antagonists and want to triumph.

Color: red and blue

Day of the week: Thursday

Drinks: dry rum

Planet: Jupiter and Mars

Food offers and gifts: the same as in Danbhallah We Do

Seasoning: hot pepper and gunpowder

Spirits

Most magical practices that exist depend on some sort of element. In particular, they bring together water, fire, earth, and air, all four of which are commonly considered to be distinctive elements that exist. Each of these elements has power in the universe, and that is recognized in Hoodoo as well. However, it is not just those elements that we see in the world that are important. More is used, primarily in symbolism and in the connection to the earth they maintain, which is important. In hoodoo, most of the elements that we use will help us connect to the spiritual realm. They are there to help us bridge that gap to start to communicate with the spirits. It requires a degree of symbolism, which you will start to see throughout the coming chapters. And we will also see that the symbolism and representative magic is incredibly beneficial.

Ancestral Spirits

Ancestral magic refers to the DNA that you inherited from those who came before you. It refers to the connections that you have, the essence and spirits of those who came before you. Your descendants will share that connection with you. That lineage is incredibly powerful, and when you can identify it and start to tap into it actively, you can start seeing the power that you have. However, this sort of blood magic is not without risk. There is always a chance that there is a curse causing you to pay for something from the past. Think of karma—you reap what you sow. Sometimes, however, your ancestors reap what you sow as well.

Someone with a terrible temper may actually have family members with terrible tempers as well. That temper was inherited in genetics. However, other traits that are a bit more intangible can also be passed down. Some people are particularly fortunate. Others may find themselves suffering from a curse. Ancestors who have done something that was so good or so bad that it impacted their descendants can create ties of blessings or curses to their blood. This power matters. While you personally may have never done anything that would warrant being treated poorly, the truth is, someone else in your past may have.

Similarly, however, you have the power that is passed down. Your power that you draw on comes from your ancestors. And, if you fail ever actively to acknowledge it, you can wind up in situations that are very undesirable for you. Your power can slowly wane over time as it is not acknowledged, fizzling out until it is barely there.

Your ancestral spirits are with you at all times. They are present, and they will try to guide you if you give them a chance. If you ignore them, they may not be particularly open to you, but they are there. Remember, they are more powerful than you. They are more experienced than you. They have wisdom that they can share with you. They can help you make choices that will help you, but that requires you to actually acknowledge them. That requires you to be there in positions where you can and will be able to make choices that will help you.

When you are able to start making those connections to your ancestors, you start seeing that you are capable of so much more. You start recognizing that you have that power within yourself and that you can call upon that power whenever you might need it. Before you know it, you have got that power. You are going to be able to call upon your ancestors when you need them, and they will be there for you if you have given them that connection to you and you have begun to honor them as well.

Spirits of the Roots

Hoodoo is known as rootwork, thanks to the bulk of what you do will be connected to the plants, roots, and herbs that you use. They will help you to focus on. They will help you to start channeling your power where you need it. These herbs are meant to be beneficial spiritually and physically as well, and many of these herbs also serve very medicinal purposes. As you will start to see in the next chapter, there are many different options based upon each plant's powers and properties that you can see.

Remember that, once upon a time, we didn't have a bottle of Tylenol we could take to cure our headaches—we had herbs. We didn't have law enforcement to call and serve a restraining order to protect us—we had our spiritual guides, ancestral spirits, and the rituals that we could perform to try to sway the world's fate so we could be protected. This is imperative to remember.

We have always found ways to figure out what we need. We have always known that the earth provided us with a way that we could heal our bodies, and we turned to the earth to provide us with guidance in other ways as well. The plants that were around us were there to help us. Some were even able to help us bridge that gap and connect with the spirit world. By learning which plants will help you to bridge that gap, you can start reaching out to the spirits to ensure that you have that help.

Knowing which plants will help us create the effects that we need or desire will help us become more powerful. It will help us to be able to get those effects that we want. From being able to cast protection to draw luck or goodwill, we start to see that we have the power to do what we need. We start to know which roots will do what and how that can help us to be able to cast the spells that we seek to get the effects that we need.

Spirits of the Earth

There are also spirits of the earth that must be acknowledged as well. We are not just drawing from our ancestors and the roots that we've chosen—we are also drawing from the earth's spirits. By drawing soil or other earth from the ground of locations, you can start creating the effect you want. The soil that you choose will have the properties of the place that you drew it from. A bank, for example, would bring about wealth. A casino may bring luck. A courthouse may bring justice, and earth from a crime scene may evoke evil. The earth that we use can help us to ground our spells—it works to start focusing and balancing out the magic that we draw from.

Because magic is so incredibly powerful, it can be volatile as well. However, being able to stop and connect that to the earth helps you to make sure that it is more focused. Adding soil can also help you to hone the spell that you are using. Adding that soil can actually help you direct the spell to where you want it to go. The love spell that you might want to work on could be more focused if you used soil from somewhere good to help hone it. The spell for justice might be better if you add in the soil from the courthouse that you will be in. These nuances will help protect you; they help guide the power you are drawing from so you know that it will go the direction you want. This will be enough to help you successfully navigate these different situations that you are in.

The earth also brings with it more as well. It brings with it the wealth of the universe as well. Think about it—gold comes from the earth. Gemstones come from the earth. This need for energy surrounds the world around us, and when you draw from it, you start to attract wealth as well.

The Spiritual Practices of Hoodoo

The Hoodoo spiritual practices are a component of the spiritual beliefs of the Hoodoo faith. In teachings concerning the spiritual world, practitioners may or may not use such tools as rituals and prayer. Visualization of the outcome and will of the effect and the magnetizing of the individual's or object's physical presence may be used. Prayers and offerings may be made with the help of ancestors or gods. Magic, rituals and spells, conjuring and curses conjured by the application of Hoodoo are believed to be ways of forcing change. Hoodoo is linked to sorcery and is therefore understood to promote a variety of spiritual practices and rituals. Indeed, some of these practices and rituals are found in Voodoo and other religious ritual and practices called "pagan" or "sorcery." Hoodoo is understood to be a form of Santeria practice which is an aspect of African origins. Only in North America and in the Caribbean is it called Hoodoo. Hoodoo is known to be a part of Egyptian traditions. Hoodoo might have been a part of Voodoo practice in the US. The practice of Hoodoo has roots in African American folklore and folk religion. It draws from African-American folk practices and perhaps its culture. It draws from the mysticism of the Caribbean, Native American, and European magical beliefs. Hoodoo is a spiritual practice that blends rootwork, conjures, and folk healing.

<u>**How to Get In Touch with Spirits**</u>

How do you get in touch with spirits? When you are a worship leader, people are mainly looking to you for power or guidance. There are rituals, such as making a sacrifice from things such as food, water or something people value or make use of. In most cases, the transactions with the spirits are paid for in some type of currency. The leaders make the sacrifice and then give the blessings to the people. This is why they make the sacrifice.

Hoodoo is similar to other secret societies, especially the kind that has its history in the African diaspora. However, unlike most secret societies, Hoodoo is open to the general public. With its origins being a secret African culture, Hoodoo keeps some rituals or beliefs secret from prying eyes, especially those who have no honor or respect for its traditions. It is very similar to the secret societies of the 18th and 19th centuries, like the Masonic orders and Catholic and Anglican institutions. The only difference is in what these secret societies believe in, which is their spiritual and religious philosophies. If something is revealed, they will banish the one who reveals them and punish the one who committed the crime and broke the law.

Hoodoo rituals and traditions are similar to West African traditions. The secret masters that are in the Hoodoo tradition have African origins. The origins of Hoodoo or the African magic scene come from African countries in the context of the slave trade. Hoodoo, or African magic, especially those rituals that are performed, are based on African beliefs and philosophy. The Hoodoo tradition is a form of religion that is like other African traditional religions. The adherents of the religion believe in spiritual beings and sacred ancestors.

The ancient African philosophical and religious beliefs do not require the belief in a God or a theistic form of theology. However, many African philosophies and religions display some type of theistic theme. The prominent in African traditional religions is the presence of the Supreme Being which is assisted by lesser spiritual beings. Although In some, there is none. But in almost every African traditional religion, the concept of a Supreme Being exists, appearing in the form of a sky-god or a creator god. Not all the concepts of a Supreme Being are considered to be omnipotent.

How to Evoke Spirits in Hoodoo

In the Hoodoo tradition and African philosophy, the use of spiritual and magic spirituality is formed from the inter-relationship with the natural elements of the universe. It is not a Christian or a Judeo-Christian belief. The Hoodoo tradition believes that spiritual beings exist and that they are a part of the spirit world. In the African and Hoodoo tradition, there are many object-based rituals whose purpose is to make contact with spirits to make a transaction or a trade. An example of how that is related to Hoodoo tradition is the burning of incense and other herbs used to aid in the invocation of a spirit. Another example would be the burning of oils or candles in a ritual, like using a candle as a focal point. Hoodoo is a pact between humans and unseen counterparts, or higher beings in the spirit world to establish a deal or a transaction between humans and spirits.

In Hoodoo, spiritual or magical work is the making of deals with one of these higher beings to exchange services. The service could be doing rituals like candles offered to the spirit in exchange for a wish.

Hoodoo is not just using spiritual work for rituals but also for love or even to talk to spirits for guidance and advice when you are having problems in your relationship or marriage. In Hoodoo, if you have problems with a partner or questions about love, you can talk to a spirit who will help and guide you to a solution for your problems. In Hoodoo, spirit guides are called Orisha, Odu or Obayifo.

CHAPTER 13: IMPORTANCE OF CROSSROAD

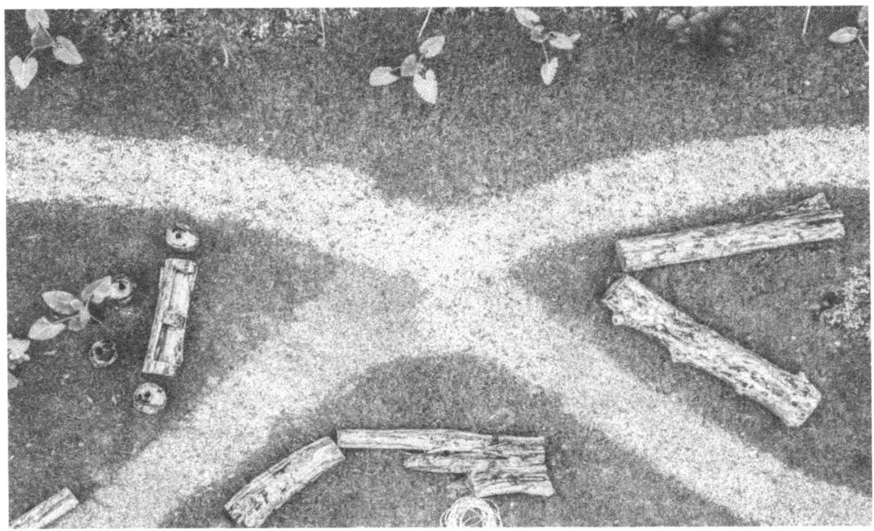

Crossroads also represent an important element to Hoodoo magic. In particular, when we see crossroads, we acknowledge that there is an opportunity. Think about it—when you stand at the center of a crossroads, you can see that there are four different directions you can go. You have opportunities, and those opportunities that present themselves are incredibly powerful as well.

You can use these to start casting off bad energy. You can use them to protect yourself and to create the effect of encouraging transition. However, unlike a graveyard, a crossroads doesn't have to carry that same air of death that you would otherwise see.

Additionally, the crossroads represent a place of magical neutrality. This makes it commonplace for your spell remnants to be disposed of. If you have created a spell using supplies that is very magically powerful, you may want to neutralize the power in the remnants by leaving them at a crossroads. This will help to lower the power that they have so that they can be disposed of safely.

The junction, also known as "the crossroads," is where two paths intersect at right angles. It is the topic of religious and folkloric beliefs throughout the world. Because the junction is a piece of land that belongs to no one and is located outside the city limits, it is seen as a good location for conducting magical rites and casting spells. Using the crossroads as an improvised altar where offerings are deposited, rituals are commonly conducted in European and African folklore.

Almost every ethnic group in Africa has its own version of the deity of crossing. Legba, Elegbara, Ellegua, Eshu, Exu, Nbumba Nzila, and Pomba Gira are names of the spirit that leads the way, protects the crossroads, and imparts knowledge in African and African diaspora languages.

Some contemporary anthropologists have christened these crossroads gods as delinquents. This, in my opinion, is a misnomer because not all gods and spirits of crossbreeds are cheaters (untrustworthy, clever, deceptive), and not all cheating gods or spirits are gods of the crossroads.

Crossbreeding beliefs in the United States are diverse and varied. There are two major themes concerning crossroads rituals in the African American hoodoo tradition. While these practices may contain elements of European folklore, they are mostly descended from African ancestors.

After finishing a "magical work" or magical ritual, the most neutral method to dispose of remnants such as candle wax, incense ash, dirt, or ritual bath water is to carry everything to the crossroads, dump everything into the crossing, then turn and go home without looking back.

(Alternative ways to dispose of ritual materials include dumping them into rushing water to escape or move spells, taking them to a cemetery for hard labor against an opponent, or burying them in your own lawn to draw influences.)

If a Follow Me Boy spell is worked on to unite two individuals passionately, the trick may be tracked to every crossing between the practitioner's house and the lover's house, i.e., each crossing will be marked with ritual objects for cementing or gluing. In contrast, in at least one variation of Hot Foot or Drive Away Spell, ritual objects are hurled into a succession of junctions that leave the Citta, pushing the despised person out of the city and acting as guards against his return. There is also a variant of the junction in which Graveyard Dirt is buried at a crossroads.

Not all Hoodoo rituals take place at a true crossroads, but when tricks may be performed when casting spells, many practitioners utilize what is known as a "portable crossbreed" or circle with a cross within, known as an "X" or "cross" in general. The cross can be drawn on the ground or a personal altar with purchased or homemade powders, or it can be constructed delicately, with only five points instead of two crossed lines. In the latter situation, the points are put in the four corners where the intersecting lines meet the perimeter of an imaginary circle and at the circle's intersection or center point. If drawn this way, it is not called a crossroads, but a "five-point," a "quincunx," and some anthropologists use the term "cosmogram." In real conversations with real practitioners, you will hear them say things like this: "arrange the salt at the four corners and in the center, like point five of the die "or" sprinkle your powders in the shape of a cross mark inside a circle "or" they would place the powders near the door

The technique is documented in a 19th-century pen and ink sketch titled "the hoodoo dance" by EW Kemble. By looking closely, you will see a clearly marked portable intersection or five points in the center of the dance floor: a piece of cloth is spread out on the ground, and at the 4 corners of the cloth are placed four candlesticks with lighted candles, plus four identical pieces of herbiage judging by their size and shape, four large clematis flowers, or four carefully opened banana (plantain) peels. A little dish filled with herbiage, likely an offering, sits in the center of this portable crossing.

Crossroads is the most common location for performing a special crossroads ritual hoodoo to learn a talent, like playing a musical instrument or becoming skilled at tossing dice, dancing, public speaking, or anything you desire. According to how this ritual is commonly described, you bring the object you want to master, such as a banjo, guitar, violin, deck of cards, or dice, and wait at the junction for three or nine predetermined nights or mornings. On successive trips, you may notice the strange appearances of various creatures. A "huge black dude" will appear on your last visit. If you are not terrified and do not flee, he will request that you borrow the object you desire to learn. He will demonstrate the proper technique to utilize the item alone. When he returns it to you, you will find yourself unexpectedly endowed with the gift of greatness.

The individual who meets them at the crossroads and teaches them the skills is sometimes referred to as "the devil." He is also referred to as "the knight," "the hilarious little guy," or "the large black man," where black is the true hue and not a brown-skinned ("colored" or black) person. It is a common academic conception to equate the crossroads "devil" with Legba because it shares qualities and derives from several African crossbreed spirits (of which Legba, Ellegua, Elegbara, Eshu, Nbumba Nzila, and Pomba Gira are some African names and African diaspora), but this is completely unheard of in popular oral tradition.

This African-originated crossroads ritual is one of the most widely dispersed superstitions in African American folklore, and it is conducted across the southern states.

Who Was Tommy Johnson, Not Robert Johnson

The crossroads ritual is now most well-known in American popular culture due to the recent adoption of a bogus legend in which famed 1930s blues musician Robert Johnson claimed to have learned to play the guitar by selling his soul to the devil at the crossroads, somewhere in Mississippi. Indeed, the blues artist who made this public claim was Tommy Johnson, a lesser-known contemporary and friend of Robert's who was unrelated to Robert. Tommy Johnson is widely known for his iconic version of "Maggie Campbell Blues." Tommy Johnson's brother, LeDell Johnson, spoke with blues researcher David Evans about Tommy's newfound ability to play the guitar and his claims. His description of the ritual is typical of other crops in the south.

It's worth noting that LeDell made no mention of Tommy Johnson calling the crossroads ghost "the devil" or selling his soul.

"Get a guitar and head towards a crossroads where the road meets the other road if you want to learn to write songs on your own." Get there, and make sure you arrive before 12 a.m. that night, so you know you'll be there. You have your guitar and perform a solo piece there. A huge black man will come up and take your instrument and tune it. Then he'll play a piece for you and hand it to you. That's how I learned to play anything I wanted." from David Evans' "Tommy Johnson" (London: Studio Vista, 1971).

In blues mythology, the crossing of highways 49 and 61 in Mississippi is explicitly mentioned as the location where many artists went to sell their soul to the devil (or, as we know it, Legba) in return for powers beyond this world and recognition.

The Hoodoo is a belief system in and of itself, and the ritual of acquiring skills at a crossroads is simply one of the hundreds of activities that comprise the Hoodoo heritage. Robert Johnson worked on the Hoodoo and believed in it, but he never claimed to have utilized the crossroads ritual to learn the guitar. That's not to say he didn't; many others did, and not only to learn to play the guitar, but also to become adept on other musical instruments, develop their dancing talents, and become good.

To play a dice game and learn acrobatics (casting spells). In the spirit of completeness, I must reiterate that Robert Johnson never claimed to have completed the crossing ritual.

Hoodoo was and still is a widely held concept among African American communities. It is not a "cult," there is no "initiation," and it is something that may be "picked up" by family members, neighborhood storytellers, and even newspaper advertisements.

The customary colors ascribed to the spirit of the African crossroads are red and black, and gifts of wine and slaughtered animals are made to the same spirit, making it easy for Christian slaves and their masters to mistake it with "the devil" (e.g., example Satan, the adversary to monotheistic god in the Jewish, Christian and Islamic religions). The spirit of the crossroads, however, is not Satan. He is also not the Judeo-Christian devil because he is malevolent, hurtful, deceiving, or harsh. He is a spiritual being who is worshipped by a polytheistic religious system. It does not need the use of "dark arts" in the medieval European sense to invoke him or gain his favor. He is a teacher and a guide who shows the path.

Crossbreeds are considered to respect in both Hoodoo and Voodoo because they serve an important part in setting the stage for various ceremonies, rituals, and requests. Ritual residues may be disposed of at the crossroads, spiritual hot springs can be disposed of, curses can be lifted, and various spells can be performed and increased.

The Crossroads and the Black Man

Another well-known place in the practice of hoodoo is the crossroads. The "X" crossroads, in particular, has a deep meaning. It is the center of the world, the place from which all roads depart, the place from which all corners of the world can be seen. It is a ritual place par excellence, full of power and inhabited by powerful spirits. This fascination was also well known in European antiquity, which placed at the crossroads the newsstands of the family lari and the god Mercury, which later became the Italian Madonnas and saints.

The Madonna or the saint probably have been there since the year 500, the newsstand probably since 300 before Christ. The crossroads in the hoodoo is the subject of legends, pacts with the spirits, and the favorite place of a particular character: the black man. He is often confused with the devil and is also called the devil or Satan, but the root doctors know that there is nothing more different. The black man or man of the crossroads is an archetypal character, present in many cultures of the world, in particular, it is important in African religions and practices and those that derive from them. He is known by many names: exu, eleggua, papa legba, maitre carrefour, calfu, lucero mundo are just some of them. In some religions and philosophies, he is a deity, in others an ancestor with great powers but he is always linked to four things: change, crossing, divination and play. He is considered as a joker spirit, lover of parties, gambling, who enjoys making jokes and is often considered the link between the gods and man.

To it are given honors and offers before the other spirits and, in hoodoo, is the only spirit that has a dedicated ritual, the ritual of crossing, which allows the person who performs it to make a pact with him. This pact brings good luck to those who contract it, it can be used to have fame or skill. The thing that makes this spirit darker and more interesting is the fact that it never refuses a desire of whatever nature it is. It is the contact with our deep unconscious, with the unexpressed desire, with our true moral essence. Both the intersection and the black man cannot be explained, they can only be perceived. Here comes into play the gnosis, the intuition of the sacred, and the personal sensitivity of the individual.

The Crossroads Ritual

While visiting the crossroads every night, you may or may not see or be greeted by any number of black animals. On the last night, you will be greeted by a figure. It could be a person dressed in black, it could be a black man (i.e., a person of African origin); however it appears, it will be the Devil. If you show no fear, he will take the object you have brought to you and teach you how to use it correctly. Finally, he will return the object to you, and you will have both the mastery and the ability to use the object.

CHAPTER 14: SPELLS

The Hoodoo spells

The Hoodoo spell is more properly called an oath and, in its substance, is as varied as one can imagine. It can be classified according to the action that you want to undertake and we speak of averts of blessing, curse, money, love, power, health, justice. Often they are also classified according to the association of traditional "color": white for the blessing, black for the curse, green for money, red for love, purple for power, blue for health, brown for justice. The curses of blessing include all exorcisms that seek to remove bad spirits, purify people or environments, attract good spirits, those of curse include the real curses, revenge, removal, punishment of evil tongues and troublesome characters, those of money seek to bring economic benefits or luck at the game; those of love have to do with "ligaments," attract love, cement the couple or help to find a new lover; those of power seek to make some people be subject to others; those of health seeks to heal diseases or accelerate the healing; finally those of justice include all actions aimed at winning lawsuits or have advantages in court.

Of course, all these categories are not precise and insurmountable distinctions, and often new ones are created depending on the situation and the action sought. To perform them, you can use herbs, prayers, powders, oils, bags, stones, dolls, animal remains, and objects among the most varied. These "tools," unlike other techniques and magical philosophies, do not have a precise form and there are not indispensable. There are no knives, sticks, cups consecrated for a certain symbolism rather than for another; often in fact the root doctor acts with what he has at the moment.

Let us remember, in fact, that the Conjure man of the past often did not have the possibility to resort to elaborate symbolic solutions, nor to read traditional texts, nor did he have enough time to devote to study and preparation. Everything was entrusted to his brain and to his knowledge of the tradition. With time things have changed, but the characteristic simplicity of Hoodoo remains the same. A kitchen stocked with a few spices and a piece of cloth, some soil taken from a special place, an oil made by infusion, a candle, a bible can give acceptable solutions for many a two-headed doctor.

Love Spells

<u>Honey Jar Spell</u>

What You Need

- Pen and paper

- Slate to place your candle on

- Pink or red candles

- Your preferred love herbs and roots like cloves, rose petals, cardamom, and magnolia

- Attraction oil or powder

- Jar with honey in it

Instructions

Honey is often used to attract other people because that is its natural state. Bees are drawn to honey and nectar, and so it will attract love. In ancient days honey was also used as offerings to love and fertility deities to access their gifts.

Take the piece of paper and write the name of the person you want to reconnect to three times. Now rotate the paper and write your name three times, so it overlaps their name and forms a block. Circle the block with loving words and phrases like "love me" and "come back to me" without lifting your pen from the paper.

Now add the oils and herbs to the paper. You can add some personal items to strengthen your honey and infuse it with your intentions. Use hair from your heads or even bodily fluids (use your imagination here) to enhance the mix. All these items should be kept in the center of the paper.

Now charge the jar with herbs, roots, and other items related to loving. Rosemary represents fidelity, while orange peel signifies joy. Use your favorite ingredients to charge the honey before you add the paper.

Now place the paper into the honey jar while reciting the following words "This honey is sweet to me just like (say the name of the person you are influencing) will be sweet and loving to me."

Place your candle on the slate and use the honey from the jar to anoint it. Light the candle and ask for help from the spirits and deities of love. Repeat for three days, and the spell will be cast.

Finding Love with Honeysuckle

What You Will Need

- Love Drawing Oil

- Red candle

- Honeysuckle flowers

Instructions

Dress the love candle with the Love Drawing Oil by rubbing the oil on it from top to bottom.

Place the candle on a plate on a non-flammable part of your altar.

Sprinkle the petals of the honeysuckle flowers around the candle wick and then light it.

Center your focus on your intentions (to attract your true love) as you watch the flame burn.

This work draws on your energy and focus. You will focus on the flames, visualize your intentions, vocalize your expectations in the form of the scriptures, and then will them into existence. You must stay at the candle until you can smell the scent of the honeysuckle, and then let the candle burn down naturally. You can speak the Song of Solomon 2:10-13 to aid the work as the candle burns.

Pinning Your Partner Down

What You Will Need

- Hoodoo doll

- Tailor pin (for a man)

- Candle (for a woman)

- Holy water

- Pubic hair of the target

Instructions

Place the pubic hair of the target on the doll for potency. The pubic hair should be placed on the corresponding genital area of the doll.

Bind the doll to the target by sprinkling the doll's head thrice with holy water and repeating these words, "I name you (insert target's name). You are now this doll and this doll is you."

For a man, pierce the genital area of the doll with the pin, but make sure it doesn't go through the doll. Then tell the doll what you want.

For the woman, place the genitals of the dolls over a burning candle. Call her name three times and speak your intentions to the flames. Don't let it burn. The result might be permanent.

Keep the doll in a safe space.

Whenever you want to have intercourse with your partner, take out the pin for the man. For the woman, place a ball of wet cotton wool on the doll's genitals. Relations should proceed as usual. When they go out, and you suspect their intentions, simply run through steps 3 or 4 and then repeat step five.

Money

The Money Spell

What You Need

- A green candle

- A white candle

- Prosperity oil like bergamot, eucalyptus, or jasmine

In this spell, the green candle represents wealth and money, and the white candle represents you. To maximize the power of the spell, you can inscribe the white candle with your name.

Instructions

Charge your candles with the oil you have chosen

Place them on your altar nine inches apart

Light them both and repeat the following chant *"Money and wealth come to me."*

In fullness and in plenty three times three

I seek enrichment without harming none

With your help, it will be done

"Money, I welcome you three times three."

Move the two candles one inch closer to each other

Extinguish the candles

Repeat the ritual for nine days

On the ninth day, let the candles burn to wax before wrapping the remains in a white cloth and placing it in your mojo bag or wallet.

Spell for Business Growth

What You Need

- A large plate
- ¼ cup of curd
- Seven coins (include some foreign coins)
- Red mojo bag
- Fast luck oil
- Almond oil
- One green, yellow, red, and blue candle
- A small magnet

Instructions

First, write the name of your business on a piece of paper and place it under the plate. If you don't have a name yet, write what your intentions and dreams for the business involve.

Place the green candle at the top of the plate, the yellow to the right, the blue to the left, and the red at the bottom. Place the magnet in the center of your candles, then light the green candle.

Pray to the gods and goddesses of plenty and ask for their assistance. Now light the yellow candle and repeat your prayers. Follow this with the red and blue candles.

Once the candles have burned down, take the remnants of the curd, the wax, and the coins and place them in your red mojo bag. Carry it with you wherever you go. The spell should be reenergized and repeated every six months or whenever you feel the need.

Remember, there are no freebies in business. All exchanges should be equal, and you need to keep yourself energized. This doesn't mean you can't be generous or helpful but don't overextend yourself or be overly generous.

<u>**The Green Candle Money Spell**</u>

What You Need

- A green candle

- Six coins, two gold, two silver, and two bronze

- A gold cloth

- Jasmine oil

Instructions

Prepare your altar and take a moment to pray to your favorite deity. Ask for assistance in your magic work, and pray for success. Once you feel charged with energy, begin the spell.

Anoint the candle with your oil and place it in the center of your altar.

Place the six coins around the candle to form a circle of alternate-colored coins, as you prepare the candle and coins, visualize what you will do with the money or good fortune your spell will attract.

Light your candle while repeating the phrase below three times

"Make the money flow and make my fortunes grow. As the money shines, god fortune will be mine."

Lay out the gold cloth and place the six coins on it. Form a pouch from the cloth while repeating this phrase *"Money comes three by three; all good fortune come to me."*

Carry the pouch with you wherever you periodically charge it with your favorite herb or oil to make it work.

Protect Your Business Mojo Bag with Devil's Claw

What You Will Need

- 1 tablespoon Devil's Claw root, dried or powdered

- 1 teaspoon Dried five finger grass - to ward off evil

- 1 teaspoon Goldenseal root - for protection

- Money Drawing Oil

- Piece of paper

- Pen

- Green cloth

- Twine

Instructions

On the piece of paper, write down your business's name along with your intention. Something like, "Stop people from stealing from me."

Pour 7 drops of Money Drawing Oil on the paper.

Put the herbs on top of the petition paper and fold it closed as best you can.

Wrap the paper with the green cloth.

Secure the green cloth with a twine.

Put it in a safe location in your business.

A mojo bag is a small spirit and must be fed. You should feed the mojo bag regularly with either rum, Hoyt's Cologne, or holy water. A few drops once per week should do. Each time you feed it, remind the spirit inside what you want it to do.

Dream Home Purchase with Shoes

What You Will Need

- 1 green candle

- 1 yellow candle

- 2 pieces of paper

- Pen

- Favor Cologne

- A pair of shoes (yours)

-

Instructions

Write down the address of your dream home on each of the pieces of paper.

Dress the papers with the Favor Cologne.

Insert each of the pieces of paper in each shoe.

Walk around the building you want to buy nine times, then return home.

Remove the paper from each shoe and set it aside.

Light both candles at your altar.

Burn the papers in the flames of these candles, one piece of paper per candle.

After you've finished, dispose of the tools for the spell in running water.

Please note that this spell is meant to be carried out before you place the bid on the house. You can put the papers into your shoes before doing a walk-through and then walk around the house nine times as part of that process.

Success

Success by Invoking: A Simple Candle Spell

You will need

- Scissors or something sharp to carve with.

- Crown of success conjure oil.

- Your intent.

Instructions

Cleanse all of your materials. Carefully carve your name and date of birth into the candle using a sharp end of the scissors (or whatever you have to carve with).

On the opposite side of the candle, or underneath your name, carve in what it is that you want. If your petition is a little long for a candle, try editing it down to a couple of words, such as 'dedicated subscribers.'

Anoint your candle with the crown of success oil, making sure to go from the bottom and upwards. Cover the wick, your name, and the petition with your fingers, which should have the oil on them.

Add your essence by speaking your intention into the candle before lighting it. Once it's lit, recite the Psalms and express gratitude. You can also speak to the flame and put into it everything you want.

This is something you want to think about *before* casting your spell: the type of problems that will follow when you achieve. Do you want these problems? Speak your anxieties or worries about achieving success to the fire. Ask Spirit and your ancestors for help with all that will come as your star rises.

Continue burning the candle until it goes out on its own. If you achieve your goal before the candle is finished, you can stop doing the daily ritual. I like to let the candle burn out on its own one last time and use the light as a reminder to keep a gratitude attitude.

If the candle goes out before you achieve what you're looking to achieve, consider the spell complete. Whenever you think about the spell or catch yourself worrying about results, remind yourself that you did the spell and the work is done.

I can understand the temptation to do another spell but do your best to resist doing another work. This will undermine the candle spell you've already done and undermine your magick overall.

You can, however, *continue* the work by anointing yourself with a crown of success oil or burning the oil with an herb in a homemade incense.

When you speak about whatever you cast for, speak as if what you want has already happened, especially if you are speaking to yourself about what you want.

Never think of the spell as having "not worked." (It's fair to say this goes for any spell you do.) If what you wanted did not happen, think of how you can do things better next time. Or better yet, think of how the spell worked in any unexpected ways.

Prosper Me Pumpkin Spell

If you want to get some more luck into your home, you want to bring in some of the luckiest things that you can. In this spell, you will be working with a pumpkin, pecans, ginger, brown sugar, and rum to create a spell that will not only smell amazing as you work through it but will start bringing good luck, prosperity, and love into your home. Are you ready? This spell is quite simple. You will just do the following:

Start by cutting open your pumpkin carefully. You are leaving the seeds inside of it.

Then, carve the names of the people you want to be blessed with good luck into the sides of the pumpkin, right into the skin.

Put all ingredients inside of the pumpkin and toss in any personal belongings or effects of those who you want to have blessed.

Then, if possible, dig a fire pit into burning the pumpkin. You will bury the pumpkin in the soil, then have a fire on top of it while you let the fire burn. Share a meal while you want the fire to burn out.

If you can't dig a fire pit, then you can bake the pumpkin in your oven set to 200 all day long.

Bury the pumpkin either in your yard or in the nearest crossroads to get the effect intended.

Prosper Me Wash

Take two large handfuls of each of your herbs and toss them into 2 quarts of water.

Then, while you boil the water, pray Psalm 23 over your pot.

Then, take out your herbs and bury them.

Wash your floors, walls, door frames, and other surfaces of the home or business that you are trying to bless.

Do this five times over five weeks, choosing Fridays as the day of choice.

<u>**Sweeten My Business with Honeycomb**</u>

What You Will Need

- A small piece of honeycomb (to sweeten and stabilize)

- Lodestone (to attract)

- Three basil leaves (to draw money)

- Piece of green cloth

- String or twine

Instructions

Place the green cloth at the center of your altar.

Put the honeycomb at the center of the green cloth.

Put the lodestone and basil leaves on top of the honeycomb.

Wrap the green cloth to cover everything and tie it closed.

Bury the bundle close to your business or home.

This spell can also be used if you are uncertain about your job. Repeat the process mentioned here, but in the last step, bury it close to your place of work.

<u>**Restore Passion for Your Work Bath with Saffron**</u>

What You Will Need

- 1 cup Saffron

- 1 cup Patchouli (to move forward)

- 1 cup Gravel root (to bring blessings)

- A pot of water

- A stove

- Spray bottle

- A strainer

Instructions

Pour the ingredients into the pot.

Bring the water to a boil.

Let half the water boil away, then set the pot aside to cool.

Strain into a spray bottle and dispose of the herbs in running water.

In a bathtub or shower, wash the water over yourself. Take your time, and think of the parts of your work that you actually like, or liked when you first started.

You can enhance the bath by reciting Psalm 23 while you wash. Before leaving for work, spray on some of the Favor Cologne to help bring you good fortune.

Peace

End Conflict with Sugar

What You Will Need

- 1 teaspoon Sugar

- 1 teaspoon Vanilla extract (to calm troubles)

- A few drops of lavender essential oil (for luck in love)

- A small blue candle

- A jar filled with water

Instructions

Pour a few drops of lavender oil, vanilla extract, and sugar into each hole.

Place the candle at the center of your altar and light it.

Speak your intentions as the candle burns.

When the candle burns out, put the candle ends inside the jar of water.

Seal the jar tightly and bury it in your backyard.

Blue candles are used for bringing healing to relationships. When your relationship is gripped with strife, putting an end to the conflict is one way to put things back on track and restore peace. When the sealed jar goes into the ground, so does the conflict. When you cover it with dirt, the conflict is as good as gone. Do not break this jar. You can enhance the work with Psalm 32.

Psychic Peace Spell

To create it, you will need:

- 1 orange peel

- ¼ cup honey

- 3 cups of pomegranate juice

- 3 lemongrass stalks

Instructions

Start by boiling the juice, honey, orange, and lemongrass until the liquid starts to thicken a bit.

Pray Psalm 10 over the mixture while you stir counterclockwise.

Pray Psalm 4 over the mixture, stirring clockwise.

Drink before bed each day for the next nine days. You should be able to prevent any sort of unwanted spiritual connection.

For Your Space: A Knot Spell

You will need

String in a 'peace' color (see candle options above) or any type of string that is strong enough to withstand being tied into knots (i.e., not sewing thread). Twine is an excellent, neutral option.

Your petition and statements.

Instructions

Cut your string long enough so you can tie nine knots, and then double this over so you have one end that is a loop.

This spell is really about item #2. You want to have your intention so clear in your mind, that when speaking freely your words match up with what you want. This spell is about solidifying what you want as your hands tie each knot.

Tie three knots, close together making your statements. Then three more, and then the last three doing the same.

Your petition does not have to be the same for each knot. For example, for the first knot in this spell you may say something as simple as: *Peace now for me and my space.* The second knot: *Serenity now for me and my space.* The third: *Inner stillness for me and my space.*

If you need to be even quieter, you can say these in your mind, pray or meditate on what you want.

Protection

<u>For Your Self: A Loving Protection Oil</u>

You will need

- A black candle

- A glass bottle

- Cinnamon sticks (you will be using one, make sure it can fit in the glass bottle)

- Pink salt

- Castor oil

- Dried rose petals

Instructions

Another simple spell, for this one we're going to layer the ingredients inside the bottle, starting with the cinnamon stick. You can follow the order above for the rest of the items.

You may also want to use Holy Water for this spell by putting some on your hands and sprinkling it around your space. This is optional.

The one "item" I did not include on this list is *you*. Before putting the cap on your bottle, add something of yourself to the spell. This can be some of your hair, nails, blood, or spit.

A resin-like Myrrh is both healing and protective and associated with Mother Mary or the goddess Isis. An essential oil like rosemary can lend both cleansing and protective properties to your oil. It is spiky and has the ability to encourage clarity.

You don't need to add either of these to your bottle; this is where I encourage you to get creative.

As much as you might want to, do not use the oil right away. Let it sit for at least two weeks before using it. Let your work rest in a dark space away from sunlight (a medicine cabinet is perfect).

Power and Protect Hand Spell

You will need the following:

- High John Root

- Urine from your target (or cologne if you can't get urine)

- Red thread

- Name paper

- Salt

Instructions

Start by writing the target's name on paper. If you are the one being protected, then you are the intended target. Then, after you have the name paper, soak it with urine or cologne.

Cover the paper with a sprinkle of salt. Then, recite Psalm 91 over it.

Wrap the paper around the High John Root.

Then, bind the paper with the red thread, wrapping it around the root.

Allow the root to dry in the sun for three days. Then, carry it with you after that. Every Monday, feed it with Florida water, cologne, or more urine.

Protection from Evil Candle Spell

This spell only needs a few simple tools:

- A blue 7-day candle

- Dried onion

- Cloves

- Camphor oil

Instructions

Start by poking three holes in the top of your candle.

In one hole, drip in four drops of your camphor oil.

In the other two holes, ad a bit of each herb.

Write the name of the person, place, or thing that you want to protect onto paper and place it under the candle.

Pray Psalm 91 over your candle. Light it and burn it daily, reciting the Psalm every time you light it.

Protection from Losing Children Spell

You will need:

- Dirt from your front yard

- Dirt from a churchyard (or from a crossroads)

- Your child's shoes

Instructions

Then, when you have everything, you will put a bit of the dirt from your yard into your child's left shoe. You will take a bit of the dirt from the churchyard and sprinkle it into your child's right foot. After doing this, they should have the protection to keep them at home with you, safe and sound.

Luck

Lucky Cologne Spell

- Orange peel

- Rum

- Nutmeg

Instructions

Take your orange and your nutmeg and toss them into a full bottle of rum.

Close the bottle and shake it while chanting, "All my kin, below and above, make me lucky, and make me love."

Then, put your bottle into a sunny spot and leave it there for nine days. Every day, shake it and repeat your chant.

Use the oil on candles (making sure they're unlit first), mojos, baths, or anywhere else that you want to help bring luck and joy to your life.

Seal the Deal with Pancake Syrup

What You Will Need

- Pancake syrup

- Jar

- Brown paper

- Pen

Instructions

Put the syrup in a pan and leave it to boil. Syrup may be faster than honey, but boiling it will speed it up.

When it is bubbling, pour the syrup into a jar.

Put the person's name paper in the jar.

Store in a dark place and then go ahead with the deal.

Dispose of the jar in running water as soon as the deal is done.

To give more power to the spell, you can substitute something personal from the target instead of using a name paper. Things like pieces of their clothing, their handwritten signature, and so on would work just fine. Just swap out their name paper and follow the rest of the instructions.

Justice

For Court Cases: A Simple Fire Spell

You will need

- A white 7-day candle (it's better if you can get one specifically for the purpose of your working, in this case, going to court).

- A conjuring oil, again, anything that speaks to your work, but snake oil is a good option if you can find it from a reputable retailer.

- A copy* of the paperwork for the case.

- A black marker.

- Tobacco.

- A cauldron or plate with tin foil so you can collect ashes.

You may wonder why I'm recommending snake oil for this spell and not a court case or law stay away oil. The court case would work for this spell as well, but as a beginner, I am considering that after you cast this spell, you may have no need for a whole bottle of court case oil. On the other hand, a bottle of snake oil can be used for this and in other workings, like protection for example.

For tobacco, empty out the contents of a cigarette (use one from someone else if you don't smoke yourself). If having cigarettes is triggering for you, purchase a cigar from a local bodega.

Buying a whole pack of cigarettes just for this spell is not the message you want to send to spirit. It suggests you will have a lot in your life that you will need to do similar work on.

Approach this with a beginner's mind and just get what you need.

*You definitely want to use a copy of the court case papers because you will be burning it. Keeping the original will provide you with strong evidence when your magick works!

Instructions

Turn the paper upside down and take out your marker. Write down words that reverse whatever this case is about for you. Use your name and date of birth and continue writing words that oppose what is already on the page.

Avoid writing down anything that you desire. This is banishing magick. Everything you're using (the oil and fire, eventually) is about dissolving this situation. If you put down what you *do* want, you send confusing messages to spirit and risk including those good things within the banishing.

Think about what you want when you celebrate victory; *after* the spell is closed.

Dress your candle with the oil (place a few drops in at the top) and the tobacco. Light the candle, picturing the court case removing itself from your life.

Rip off a section of the court document copy. Rip the paper away from you.

You will rip a piece of the paper for each day of the work, so consider how many days you will do the work. Take your piece while leaving enough for each day you plan to work.

Set the paper on fire using the lit candle. Let it burn until the fire goes completely out and all that's left are the ashes.

Once all the paper has been burned, collect the ashes. In the traditional version of this spell, you would go to the courthouse and sprinkle all of the ashes there. If your case will be taking place over an online video conferencing platform, it is still possible to do this step. Remember, this work is about spirit. The correspondences still exist even as our world remains in flux.

If there *is* a courthouse address on your paperwork, use this. If there isn't an address, do a little research online to find a courthouse closest to you, even better if you can find a courthouse nearby where similar cases are handled.

Baby Daddy Spell

- Truth oil

- Tobacco leaves

- Dirt dauber nest

- Child's hair

- The name paper of the father

Instructions

Start by dressing the name paper with three dots of truth oil. Then, fold the items into the paper. Pray over it, "[Father's name]; this is your [son/daughter]. Come and lift them up!" Repeat this nine times.

Carry the packet with you and repeat your nine iterations of the prayer nine times per day for nine days.

If the father acknowledges the truth within the nine days, save the packet somewhere safe.

If he does not acknowledge the truth, bury the packet in the churchyard with a coin. This will curse his money until he supports his child.

Quick Reconciliation Spell

Are you in a bit of a tough spot with someone right now but wish you weren't? You are not alone—you can use this spell to help to heal the quarrel before it can be allowed to fester any longer. This particular spell will require you to first write out all of Psalm 32, take a pink candle, eight pins, and honey. When you have everything, you can start the spell.

Begin by writing out all of Psalm 32.

After writing everything out, write on the back of the paper, the name of the person with who you wish to reconcile, and do so three times.

Then, carve the name of the person you wish to reconcile with into the candle three times.

Place the pins around the candle on the bottom of the plate in a circle. Then, cover the pins with honey (this encourages the pain of the argument to be forgotten).

Burn over the next three days. Every day, repeat Psalm 32.

Fertility Spells

To Enhance Fertility

To enhance fertility, avoid miscarriage, and increase male potency, make a Ya-Ya powder and sprinkle it on yourself on a daily basis. You will need the listed below ingredients to make this powder:

- Vetivert

- Cinnamon

- Sage

- Rose

Take a handful of each herb and crush it into a powder. Mix well with a cornstarch base.

Making a Woman Barren

Roll the egg of a guineafowl bird in cayenne pepper and Goofer dust. Cook it in a kettle of pure rainwater until it becomes firm. This will result in the woman's infertility.

Healing Spells

To Heal Physical Ailment

You will need the listed items to cast this spell:

- A piece of amethyst (preferably as transparent as possible) or Fluorite

- Good visualization skills

Sit in a peaceful area and cleanse your mind of everything that comes to mind. Hold the amethyst (or Fluorite) in the hand that is closest to the pain (if the pain is in the center of the body, hold it in your writing hand). Imagine a calming light gathering at your feet and gently drawing it up towards your head, filling every part of your body. While doing so, silently recite the following verse:

"Shining light, bright light

Heal my hurts with all thy might."

Rep this as you move the light up your body. When you get to the top of your head, extend to cover the space around your head with light for approximately afoot. Then, return to the place of most discomfort and direct all of your healing energy there. If that does not work the first time, try again. You should start feeling better soon. To conclude the spell, repeat the poem but add "so be it."

Voodoo Doll Healing Spell

A white Voodoo doll is required for this spell since white is the color of healing and purification. On a paper piece, write the person's name in need of healing and connect it to the doll with a personal impact that belongs to the person. Set 2 white candles on either side of the doll, anointed with holy oil. Anoint the doll as well with the holy oil. Light the candles and offer your prayers for good health and healing.

CHAPTER 15: USEFUL VOCABULARY WITH WORDS USED IN HOODOO

Two-Headed Doctors

Two-Headed Doctors are those who have learned their craft from the spirit of a two-headed doctor. Stories differ on how they were born but say that the two heads give them powerful healing medicine and knowledge not only about medicinal herbs but about magic as well.

Mojo

Mojo is a powerful force in magic and is the most commonly known term for the magical working that is performed by practicing hoodoo practitioners. In many African cultures, it's thought to be an essential part of life. The word "mojo" has come to be synonymous with any magical charm or device created by a practitioner and employed for benevolent purposes.

Hoodoo

An African American folk magic belief system and magical practice.

Spiritualism

A broad Christian eschatological movement that results in modern spiritual practices and beliefs.

Grimoires

Books of magic spells were primarily written during the seventeenth through nineteenth centuries, although some date back to the thirteenth century.

Ready to use

Perhaps the easiest way to create a baby doll is to buy a store-bought doll as a generic doll or an action character. The doll should be cleaned with ammonia and incorporate the personal concerns of the individual you wish the doll to represent.

Wax Images

Many spiritual practitioners are familiar with male and female candles which are often used in candle magic spells. However, these small images can easily be used in the same way as a wax image because that is exactly what they are. To prepare a candle, like a baby doll you can simply scratch the person's name on the doll's chest.

Poppet

A poppet is composed of two pieces of cloth cut in the shape of a human body. This fabric can also be something that the individual has worn or simply a piece of colored fabric that fits your target. The pieces are sewn together, turned upside down and filled with cotton, herbs, straw, buds, **etc.** If you have a connection with the individual, add it to the inner padding. Finish by sewing the opening you used to fill it. Then, personalize the doll by giving it the characteristics of the person it is intended to represent, hair and eye color for instance. When you are finished, wrap the doll in a clean cloth until the spell or ritual has been performed.

Rootworkers

Rootworkers (also known as "Hoodoo Hands" or "Granny Women") are practitioners of American folk magic whose primary objective is the alteration of one's inner aspects and/or outer circumstances by the application of herbs, roots, minerals, oils, mojo bags and a variety of spells. Some Hoodoo workers may also curanderos in that they practice the folk healing traditions of other cultures.

Root Doctors

Root doctors known as 'hoodoo doctors' come from the practice of folk magic in African-American communities. They are called 'hoodoo' because of their use of folk magic, which is often thought to be magical. They were most prominent in the south and border states as African-Americans migrated to the north and west through the early 20th century. Hoodoo doctors were believed to help with an array of different problems, including but not limited to: love spells and potions, protection magics (such as charms for warding off evil spirits or curses), money magics (such as gris bags or mojo hands), healing charms (for healing many different ailments from minor sicknesses to major troubles such as infertility), and protection from ill wishes cast by other rootworkers via "crossing work.

Necromancy

A form of divination conducted with the aid of a necromancer or other spirit mediums, who use communication with spirits to answer questions set on behalf of others; also used as a term for rituals and incantations associated with this practice.

Sigil

A symbol is consciously constructed to represent the magician's desired outcome. Sigils are linked by belief to the details of a desired effect.

Sorcery: Witchcraft

Witchcraft:

Magic practices believed to obtain power over supernatural forces

Aggression/Assertion:

Willfully acting out or practicing spells in order to cause harm or injury upon another individual for one's own benefit.

Rootworking

Rootworkers look at plants to perform magic spells upon people or objects. They also identify herbs that may need to be planted for healing purposes.

Cross-gridding

Cross-gridders use their hands, sticks, and other items to cast spells in order to find the future and predict the unknown.

Conjure

Crowley (a renowned master of hoodoo) defined conjure as being in touch with the natural life force – a magical power that resides within all things. Some conjurers work with small objects, while others work with people or animals.

In other words, you must understand that there are no categorizations regarding who can practice hoodoo. Though it is true that most practitioners of the art fall under one of these three branches, there are also practitioners who practice mostly one craft (for instance, rootworking or cross-gridding).

CONCLUSION

Thank you for reading this book. Hoodoo is a skill, and like any skill, it takes time to become good at it. You can't get off a couch and run a marathon without a lot of practice, and you can't master the spiritual world the first time you approach your ancestor altar. You will become better with practice, I promise.

Also, remember that some spells take time. Expecting to get an immediate result after you carry out a conjure is not realistic. Some spells work very fast, but most of them require at least a few days' intervals in order to be effective.

Give it time to marinate and get going. For the most part, you are working with the help of the spirits. Your first foray into Hoodoo work is an introduction to your ancestors.

If anything, they will be delighted to have the opportunity to be involved in the affairs of your life. Enjoy the opportunities that conjure brings your way. Embrace your roots and your identity by connecting with your ancestors. This connection will empower your spells and turn you into a powerful Hoodoo worker in no time. Most importantly, enjoy yourself. Learn. Grow. Evolve.

Being a Hoodoo practitioner is more than just casting spells and changing your destiny. It is about aligning yourself with your spiritual purpose and I am thankful and honored to be a part of your process. As you close this book, meditate on some of the lessons that you have learned here. Especially the ones that deeply resonated with you. From time to time, re-read the book to find clarity on things that may not have offered enlightenment the first time you read about them. If you have friends who are equally curious, share with them the knowledge that you have gained. I believe that our world becomes a better place when knowledge is shared. Unlike the olden days, when Hoodoo was relegated to dark and mysterious corners of the world, today we are openly practicing our craft, and we are proud of it.

The purpose of Hoodoo is to give access to supernatural forces in order to improve the various aspects of everyday life such as luck, money, love, work, health or revenge. Hoodoo is practiced with the extensive use of herbs and stones and traditional ingredients of spells, fragments of animal bones, personal items and body fluids (menstrual blood, urine and semen). Very common practices in the Hoodoo magic system are contact with the spirits of the dead (including those of the ancestors) and the magical use of roots. The goal of Hoodoo is, therefore, to improve everyday life almost for medical purposes through the action of supernatural forces acting for example on love, health, in everyday life or work. Hoodoo uses the parts of animals, body parts of people such as blood, nails, hair, urine, then there are objects such as candles, incense, oil, powders used in potions.

Whatever the reason is for your interest in Hoodoo, you must use the practice with extreme care and respect. Never underestimate the power of the practices contained in this book. Thank you for reading and good practice.

The final thought is to remind you of the Law of Three, or karmic law, depending on how you define the term. Individuals who practice white magic or the right-hand path abstain from casting spells that damage, destroy, or kill. They are fully aware that the repercussions will be far too severe. After all, Hoodoo and conjure are faith-based systems with a primary focus on healing.

Good luck.